INDRA'S NET

INDRA'S NET

Alchemy *and* Chaos Theory
as
Models *for* Transformation

Robin Robertson

Theosophical Publishing House
Wheaton, Illinois * Chennai, India

Quest Books
Theosophical Publishing House
P. O. Box 270
Wheaton, IL 60187–0270

www.questbooks.net

Cover image by Diamond Art
Cover design by Kirsten Hansen Pott

Library of Congress Cataloging-in-Publication Data

Robertson, Robin.
Indra's net: alchemy and chaos theory as models for transformation / Robin Robertson.
    p.   cm.
Includes bibliographical references.
ISBN 978-0-8356-0862-6
1. Chaotic behavior in systems. I. Title.
Q172.5.C45R637 2998
003'.857—dc22   2008051949

Printed in the United States of America

5   4   3   2   1   *   09   10   11   12   13   14

To my editor, Jane Andrew, who, usually with my active agreement, though sometimes with my grumbling at the extra work, pushed me to make this a better book than it would otherwise have been. She's been the toughest (and best) editor I've ever worked with, and I hope we can work together again in the future.

Contents

Illustrations

Illustrations

Foreword

In early Taoism chaos, cosmos, becoming, time, and Tao are synonymous for that which is without an Orderer but is the "sum of all orders."

—N. J. Girardot

In the timeless mythic past of both the Western world and the Far East, chaos, creativity, and transformation were understood as forming the interwoven fabric of a spontaneous cosmos. In line with this insight, Hesiod, writing in the Greek world around 700 BC, proclaimed that the primordial yawn of chaos was not about absolute disorder and confusion, or hollow emptiness, but a richly creative space from which flowed the dual cosmic forms of heaven and earth, space filled with the power of Eros or light.

Modern science has also discovered a close relationship between chaos and creativity. Many systems in nature, and in the human sphere as well, seem to evolve through increasing levels of complexity, each bounded and set apart from the others by regions of chaos. The universe itself comes down to us from a "big bang" after which matter as we know it today consolidated through a series of distinct phases, beginning with subatomic particles and continuing to atoms and the formation of the first generation of stars. These were the flaming cauldrons in which heavy metals were created to be scattered throughout space when these stars gave up their contents in cosmic-scale explosions. These very metals became the building blocks for the large organic molecules that eventually, in turn, became the building blocks for protoplasm and cellular life. In the meantime, huge clouds of dust and gases had consolidated into galaxies filled with solar systems and planetary bodies such as our own earth. At each stage of this cosmic drama, incredibly long periods of stability were punctuated by apparent disorder, chaos, and reorganization into more complex structures.

In its own way the evolution of organic life has followed a similar path. Progress was characterized by long epochs of little change punctuated by briefer periods of dramatic experimentation, creativity, and transformation. The first organic life on earth seems to have appeared around three and a half billion years ago, but not until two billion years ago or so did the first cells with complex internal structures appear on the scene. It was well over a billion years after that when the first multicellular organisms appeared, and most complex organisms as we know them today, from reptiles and insects to mammals, have all appeared during the most recent five hundred million years. This evolutionary pathway, characterized by long periods of stability and short spurts of creative experimentation and change, is so prominent in the historical record that it is referred to as *punctuated equilibrium* by paleontologists.

We find similar patterns in the development of our own inner lives. We have all lived through periods of stability, sometimes characterized by security and happiness and sometimes by ordinary boredom, followed by intervals of chaotic transition. We see this in childhood, in which distinct "states" of growth are apparent to everyone, each with its own pattern of emotion and behavior. Then comes adolescence, a dramatic interlude of biological and mental turmoil during which the young man or woman struggles to find footing while body and mind are stretched and torn both biologically and psychologically between the certainties of past childhood and the insecurity of future adulthood.

This rhythmic movement between chaos and stasis is the hallmark of psychological transformation. It is a cycle in which old structures eventually fail to find traction in a world of increasingly complex challenges, and a sense of confusion and chaos begins to emerge. Out of this chaos, however, appear the seeds of a new and more mature organization, one with more complexity and greater adequacy for dealing with the challenges of life. The overall shape of the process is reminiscent of the alchemical stages described in this book: an earlier substance is decomposed into a more primitive and chaotic form of great potential. Out of this potential emerges the substance of great value, nothing less than the philosopher's stone, the priceless treasure extolled in alchemical lore.

Now a few words about the author. In ordinary life Robin Robertson wears many hats, not the least of which is that of a practicing magician. In the following pages he brings together his knowledge of chaos theory, his considerable experience as a Jungian psychologist, and his exceptional writing skills to create a work of remarkable literary alchemy. Perhaps no one else in the world could have synthesized so many insights from science, mathematics, history, and depth psychology, combining them with deep and abiding understanding of human nature and its many possibilities into a single lustrous thread.

Allan Combs
Santa Rosa, California
September 2008

Introduction

As the elements of the cosmos correspond to those within man,
so both the process of creation—and the process by which man,
through the Art, reintegrates himself within himself—follow an
identical path and have the same meaning.

—Julius Evola

How is it that transformation comes about? In this book, we're going to look at two models of that process, both of which ostensibly concern outer transformation, while on another level also speak about inner transformation. One is an ancient model—Western alchemy—that came into existence in the West during the first through the third centuries, reached its peak in the fifteenth and sixteenth centuries, and persisted in some form during the seventeenth and eighteenth centuries. In the nineteenth century, two writers, Mary Anne Atwood and E. A. Hitchcock, each wrote a book arguing that alchemy really dealt with the real purpose of religion: to restore mankind to the connection with divinity that existed before the Fall. In a private letter, Atwood contrasted that vision of alchemy with the mode of common religion: "The common faith is mystery without a fulcrum in this life whereon to rest the lever of the will."[1] Hitchcock said directly: "*Man* was the *subject* of Alchemy; and that the *object* of the Art was the perfection, or at least the improvement, of Man."[2] Both books are fascinating and often evince deep wisdom (though in Atwood's case that wisdom is usually overly recondite, much like the literature of the alchemists themselves). What separates those books, however, from the approach taken in this book is that they are essentially prepsychological.

1

Both assume, like many other occultists, that the alchemists consciously hid ancient, secret wisdom in difficult language and purportedly physical experiments.

It was only in 1917, with the publication of psychologist Herbert Silberer's *Problems of Mysticism and Its Symbolism*,[3] that psychology turned its lens on alchemy (and other hermetic* areas of study) as a model for psychological transformation. Silberer does not appear to have been aware of Atwood's book, of which few copies were available, and probably none in Germany, as the author and her father had withdrawn it from publication and destroyed most copies within weeks of its original publication. He was, however, aware of Hitchcock's book and drew heavily on it in some of his own interpretations. Silberer was a member of Freud's circle of therapists in Vienna. His work is a somewhat uneasy attempt to balance a Freudian interpretation of a Rosicrucian text with ideas from alchemy (in an approach similar to that of Hitchcock) and a variety of other mystical traditions. Freud rejected Hitchcock's work out of hand. Finding himself excommunicated by Freud's followers as well, Silberer hung himself.[4]

The psychological approach to alchemy was developed much more extensively by C. G. Jung, who argued that the alchemists, in their search for the "philosopher's stone," were actually seeking inner transformation. Jung called this process *individuation*. The alchemists' descriptions of their experiments could be reinterpreted as projections of the stages of the individuation process onto the physical world. In Jung's words,

> Everything unknown and empty is filled with psychological projection; it is as if the investigator's own psychic background were mirrored in the darkness. What he sees in matter, or thinks he can see, is chiefly the data of his own unconscious, which he is projecting into it. In other words, he encounters in matter, as apparently belonging to it, certain qualities and potential meanings of whose psychic nature he is entirely unconscious. This is particularly true of classical alchemy, when empirical science and mystical philosophy were more or less undifferentiated.[5]

---

* *Hermetic* refers to philosophical and spiritual traditions that trace their origins to a figure called Hermes Trismegistus, whom we will meet in chapter 2.

Mircea Eliade, the Romanian religious historian, philosopher, writer, and journalist, thought that Jung had made a major discovery, namely, that "in the very depths of the unconscious, processes occur which bear an astonishing resemblance to the stages in a spiritual operation—gnosis, mysticism, alchemy—which does not occur in the world of profane experience."[6] In contrast with Jung, however, Eliade felt that the similarities between individual and alchemical work exist because all deep mystical initiations necessarily repeat the same stages, down to the details that are buried deep in the psyche. You might say it was the alchemical path that was found within individuation, rather than the other way around, or, more properly, that a deeper process underlies both. The same phenomenon takes many guises; or, as Eliade puts it, "every symbolism is polyvalent."[7] That is largely the assumption made in this book. Eliade states the connection thus:

> The process of individuation, assumed by the unconscious without the "permission" of the conscious, and mostly against its will, and which leads man toward his own centre, the Self—this process must be regarded as a prefiguration of the *opus alchymicum*, or more accurately, an "unconscious imitation," for the use of all beings, of an extremely difficult initiation process reserved for a small spiritual elite.[8]

The other model—chaos theory—is much more recent.* It was first recognized explicitly in the early 1960s, in early computer models of weather developed by meteorologist Edward Lorenz, which we will discuss in chapter 1. His work led to recognition of a property that has been termed *sensitive dependence on initial conditions* or, more popularly, *the butterfly effect*. This metaphor, which has spread widely, originated in a question Lorenz asked in a paper delivered in 1979: "Does the flutter of a butterfly's wings in Brazil set off a tornado in Texas?"[9] The answer is yes: very tiny initial changes can have very large final effects, if the effect of the initial

---

* Throughout this book, *chaos theory* will be used as a blanket term that includes all of nonlinear dynamics, complexity theory, and similar fields. Closely related areas such as cybernetics and autopoiesis will also be discussed because, taken together, such fields present a view of nature distinctly different from previous scientific views.

changes is fed back into the system and amplified, over and over. In the words of philosophy of science professor Stephen H. Kellert: "Even in a simple system, chaos means that if you are off by one part in a million, the error will become tremendously magnified in a short time."[10]

For many people, their first exposure to chaos theory was through the book *Jurassic Park*, or its movie adaption by Steven Spielberg, in which a financier's dream of an amusement park featuring genetically recreated dinosaurs quickly turns nightmarish. In the book, one of the main characters, Ian Malcolm (played by Jeff Goldblum in the movie), gives an excellent summary of sensitive dependence on initial conditions in chaos theory. None of that description, however, made it into the movie. Though Ian Malcolm's description of the theory was somewhat muddled in the movie, the entire story was an example of sensitive dependence on initial conditions. Jurassic Park was to be the culmination of the vision of financier John Hammond (played by Sir Richard Attenborough in the film). Throughout, Hammond has an almost total confidence in the ability of science to anticipate and control every outcome. In contrast, Ian Malcolm keeps telling him (both in the book and the movie) that nature is more complex than science's models. And so it is! The plot is an unfolding of how very tiny initial differences can lead to enormously different, and unexpected, outcomes.

Alchemy and chaos theory may seem to have little in common with each other or with spiritual transformation. In fact, the two offer strikingly similar descriptions of the core processes of transformation, and each has insights about these core processes that the other lacks. It is not my intention in this book to argue that alchemy and chaos theory together provide an alternative to the many paths of spiritual transformation. Rather, I argue that anyone who is called to the difficult inner journey ineluctably awakens deep structures in the psyche that can be seen both in alchemy and, if properly translated, in chaos theory. These two parallel models provide a template for transformation, a template that underlies all other paths of spiritual transformation.

The structure of this book mirrors this template as well. After a more detailed introduction to the fundamental ideas of alchemy and chaos theory in chapter 1, in the following chapters we will discuss five critical insights that provide a framework for the stages anyone must go through on the path of individuation (to use Jung's term). Each chapter explores one insight from the perspective first of alchemy, then of chaos theory. No matter the particular spiritual path that we have chosen (or that has chosen us), these five insights can help enrich our understanding of the process of transformation, whether outside in the world or within our own lives. Thus, each chapter concludes with the lessons for self-transformation inherent within each of the following five insights.

As above, so below

In alchemy, the core belief in "as above, so below" was first presented in the fabled text known as the "Emerald Tablet" (discussed in chapter 2). This idea is no less central in chaos theory. For example, chaos theory reveals that the global (the "above") and the local (the "below") are inextricably mixed. In chaos theory, the notion that is equivalent in renown to the Emerald Tablet might be Benoit Mandelbrot's mathematical concept of fractals.

Feedback

Here I'm starting with the modern term. All of chaos theory is based on feeding information from one stage of a process to the next stage of the process. As we'll see in chapter 3, this process led to Lorenz's discovery of chaos theory. Before computers, scientists had no practical way to model the way nature continually feeds back actions into themselves. Nevertheless, alchemists tried to model such behavior by building up-and-down movements into the alchemical process through such operations as *sublimatio* (sublimation, aeration, rising, spirituality) and its counterpart *mortificatio* (mortifying, falling into matter) or the *circulatio* (continual cycles of rising and falling). But the most ancient alchemical symbol of feedback is the image of the *uroboros*, the snake that swallows its own tail.

Introduction

Take apart, put together

The practice of alchemy consists of performing a series of operations in which a developing object is taken apart and then put back together (the object will eventually become the philosopher's stone, to which we will return below). As we'll see in chapter 4, this cycle is accomplished by first performing operations such as *solutio* (dissolve) and *separatio* (break into parts), followed by operations such as *coagulatio* (coagulate, come together) or *coniunctio* (conjunction, joining). This process pervades all of chaos theory, especially in the concept of "strange attractors," to which we'll also return to in chapter 4. In chaos theory, the most famous example of "take apart, put together" is the *baker transformation*, in which a baker kneads dough over and over, separating parts of the dough that are close together and bringing together other parts that were widely separated.

Chaos and emergence

As we will see in chapter 5, the alchemical opus had three primary stages in which the varied operations took place: (1) an explicit stage of darkness and chaos: the *nigredo*; (2) a stage of whiteness and asceticism: the *albedo*; and (3) a stage in which new life emerged: the reddening or *rubedo*. Alchemists believed that because all possibilities were contained within darkness and chaos, eventually out of that chaos would emerge the philosopher's stone.

Of course, as one can tell by the name *chaos theory*, chaos is an explicit part of the modern model. As we will see in more detail, the order emerges gradually as a system *bifurcates*, splitting into first two possibilities, then four, and so on. It is impossible in advance to predict which fork the physical reality will take. Then at some further point, the bifurcations change into chaos. The new insight carried in chaos theory is that even this "endpoint" chaos has structure at a global level and that out of it emerges yet another order.

The Philosopher's Stone

In chapter 6, we turn to the alchemist's great desire: to create the philosopher's stone, or *lapis* (Latin for "stone"), which would have the power to turn ordinary metal to gold. Today we know that the true philosopher's stone is found not only outside the seeker, but also within his own soul. Alchemical texts have innumerable references to the idea that to fully carry out the *opus* (the term for the full process to produce the philosopher's stone), the alchemist must first work to purify himself and make himself worthy of the stone.

The eighteenth-century philosopher Immanuel Kant was the first to realize that we never experience *das ding in sich* (the thing in itself); rather, we experience the physical world through filters built into our inner world. Or, as expressed by twentieth-century neurobiologist Walter J. Freeman, a pioneer in the application of chaos theory within neuroscience: "Instead of minds shaping themselves to their sensory inputs from the world, minds shape sense impressions according to their innate categories."[11] Freeman arrived at this startling new conclusion through his study of dynamic attractors in the brain for odor and other senses.

This last idea—the understanding that the opus is within us as much as it is without—explains why these two models of outer transformation can teach us something about our own self-transformation. This conjoined relationship between the world and the psyche is expressed in Buddhist mythology by the image of Indra's net: a vast necklace of shining jewels, all interconnected. In the European tradition, we have the famous words of Alain de Lille, a twelfth-century French theologian: "God is an intelligible sphere whose center is everywhere and whose circumference is nowhere."[12] The message is this: each of us, through our own process of growth and transformation, affects everyone and everything.

1

The Story of Alchemy
and Chaos Theory

History is the only laboratory we have in which to test the consequences of thought.

—Étienne Gilson

I n this chapter, we are going to follow a tangled history from the development of alchemy to its near demise with the rise of science. At that pivot point stands Isaac Newton, arguably the most important person in the history of science, and also a practicing alchemist. His story will be told in the final chapter of this book, when we discuss the philosopher's stone. After Newton, science advanced into territory far, far removed from the hermetic ideas at the core of alchemy, but strangely enough, in that place, with the discovery of chaos theory, ideas similar to those of alchemy began to reappear.

A SHORT HISTORY OF ALCHEMY

The process in alchemy has always been more central than the visible results, which can only be historically and culturally defined. In that sense, alchemy belongs, with astrology, healing, and music-mathematics, to the collegiums of planet sciences that survive civilizations.

—Richard Grossinger[1]

Chapter One

Speeding Up Nature

In most histories of thought, alchemy has been presented as a primitive predecessor to chemistry. This view is a deep misapprehension, one resulting from our modern inability to understand a time when the surrounding world was still regarded as holy. The historian of religions Mircea Eliade was the first to recognize that alchemy evolved out of the mystery tradition that underlay mining and metallurgy. The men who mined and processed iron and gold and silver regarded themselves as something of a priesthood, possessed of secret knowledge about Nature (with a capital "N"). Metals were believed to be living organisms that slowly developed and changed within the body of the earth, much as a baby grows within a woman's belly. The miners who brought the ore forth from the earth, along with the metalworkers who then processed the ore, were serving as midwives who helped speed up the birth process of the metal. It's critical to understand that this belief system could arise and continue only so long as nature is viewed as alive. It is the modern scientific view of nature as a "thing" that makes this earlier view seem so strange to us. Native Americans still hold the view of the natural world as not only a living being, but a sacred living being. Increasingly, in these days of pollution and global warming, many are turning to these older traditions, no longer dismissed as primitive, for guidance on how to live in harmony with nature.

The alchemists took this tradition of metallurgical midwifery one step further, since their goal was to transform lesser elements into gold through a complex series of cyclic operations (figure 1.1). They felt that they were simply speeding up the process that took place in nature. A large part of their effort depended on heating mixtures with the proper application of fire, whether over an open flame in containers of various shapes, both functional and symbolic, or in a furnace, where the least mistake would ruin the operation. In nature, transformation of metal occurs over epochs of time through the heating of the sun or the natural heat deep in the earth; since the alchemists had to accomplish the same task in a tiny fraction of the time, they had to become masters of the processes involved. Just as nature cycles its operations over and over, feeding the results of each operation back for the next, so too the alchemist had to couple a mastery of fire with cyclic operation. In Eliade's words: "In taking upon himself the responsibility of changing Nature, man put himself in the place of Time; that which would have required millennia or eons to 'ripen' in the depths of the earth, the metallurgist and alchemist claim to be able to achieve in a few weeks."[2]

Figure 1.1. Alchemists at work.

Chapter One

Western Alchemy

In both the East and the West, the "metallurgical mysteries" evolved over time into alchemy. The first mention of alchemy may have occurred in China as early as the fourth century BC, and the art had definitely been noted there by the first century BC. Alchemy first appeared in the Western world at much the same time, at a place where West met East: Alexandria, Egypt. When Alexander the Great conquered Egypt in 330 BC, he founded the city of Alexandria. Why that location? According to Plutarch, the greatest biographer of ancient times, it was because of a dream. Alexander's favorite author was Homer, and wherever he went he carried a copy of the *Iliad*, annotated by Aristotle. One night, at a time when Alexander was considering where to build a great new Greek colony, Homer appeared in a dream to tell him to build it on an island called Pharos, on the Egyptian shore. And so he did.

Unfortunately, Alexander died before he could see the great city he had begun. But soon afterward, the Egyptian pharaoh Ptolemy I, who had been a close friend of Alexander's since childhood, created the famed library of Alexandria, the Museion, with the goal of bringing together all recorded thought in one place. It was further expanded by his son, Ptolemy II.

At its peak, the library had an enormous collection of manuscripts, which may have reached 700,000 papyrus scrolls. "The building was equipped for reading and copying, for quiet study, and for comparison of objects and specimens of the material world with the written works of the past. There is nothing quite like it in the modern world, though it must have been somewhat akin to the British Museum in London."[3] Perched as it was between the East and the West, this library offered a place where cutting-edge thinkers from all cultures could gather and share ideas that ranged across many traditions previously isolated from one another: the abstract philosophy of the Greeks for the first time intermingled with the practical metallurgical and chemical knowledge of the Egyptians and the complex mysticism of the Chaldeans and Persians. Three products of that mixture of cultures and thought were Gnosticism, Neoplatonism, and Western alchemy. These three strains of thought tended to intertwine, so that many alchemists were also Gnostics or Neoplatonists.

It was a charmed moment that didn't last. Legend has it that the library was largely burned in 48 BC, when Caesar set fire to the ships in the harbor to protect his garrison from invasion by the Macedonians. But like many legends, this one is unlikely, as several people wrote of visiting the library after 48 BC. Other accounts of the library's destruction exist and are debated among scholars. The most likely explanation for its disappearance is that most of its contents were destroyed in the third century, when the Roman emperor Aurelian invaded Alexandria, and the remaining contents and the Museion itself were destroyed over the next several centuries.[4]

Even after its partial destruction, the library remained a magnet for scholars and mystics, alchemists prominent among them. They came to Alexandria from all over the world, then left, taking with them the secrets they had learned. Many of those secrets they were forced to keep hidden, shared only with others who understood the mysteries. Muslim scholars in particular took these new ideas back to their own countries, where they flourished underground at a time when they almost disappeared in the West. When Arabs conquered Spain during the seventh and eighth centuries, Arabian alchemy moved back into the Western world. Since Spain was, at the time, also one of the central gathering places for Jews, including Jewish mystics, alchemical ideas were incorporated into Jewish mystical thought; the result was the tradition known as Qabalah.* It was only in the twelfth and thirteenth centuries, however, that these ideas spread beyond Spain to the rest of Western Europe. By the late thirteenth century, Europeans were writing their own alchemical texts, the most notable among these authors being Albertus Magnus, Roger Bacon, and Raymond Lull. In his rich book *Alchemy: The Medieval Alchemists and Their Royal Art*, Danish historian Johannes Fabricius comments on the position of the alchemists:

> Because the alchemists originated in a pre-Christian cultural world, they had to establish themselves as a subculture in medieval Christianity. Here they occupied a strange position, religiously as well as scientifically.

* There are many spellings of *Qabalah*, depending on the tradition that uses the term; these include *Qabalahh, Kabala, Kaballah, Cabala*, and many more.

The alchemists were mystics without being orthodox Catholics, scientists without following the learning of their time, artisans unwilling to teach others what they knew. They were sectarians, the problem-children of medieval society, and their contemporaries were ever hesitant about deciding whether to regard them as pure sages or sacrilegious impostors.[5]

Western alchemy reached its peak in the fifteenth and sixteenth centuries and still existed in some form during the seventeenth and eighteenth centuries (persisting underground even into our time). For example, Isaac Newton, who changed the world forever with his scientific discoveries in the seventeenth century, was a practicing alchemist who regarded his alchemical studies as being of equal or greater importance than his scientific studies. In his alchemical notes, he commented that "just as the world was created from dark Chaos through the bringing forth of light and the separation of the aery firmament and of the waters from the earth, so our work brings forth the beginning out of black Chaos and its first matter through the separation of the elements and the illuminations of matter."[6]

Newton saw no discrepancy between the two positions of alchemist and scientist. Although the world he presented in his science was a world of absolutes, he saw the deeper world revealed by alchemy as perpetually changing, constantly transforming. Mircea Eliade commented that "Newton sought in alchemy the structure of the small world to match his cosmological system"; though he was unsuccessful in his search, he remained convinced that there had been and could continue to be secret revelations about nature's most intimate secrets, "nor did he reject the principle of transmutation, the basis of all alchemies . . . In a sense the whole of his career after 1675 may be seen as one long attempt to integrate alchemy and mechanical philosophy."[7] We need to follow the winding trail that led from Newton to a science that ignored the older traditions but eventually culminated in chaos theory. But, as so often happens in the history of thought, if you scratch the surface of chaos theory, underneath you'll find the old metal of alchemical ideas, as we'll see in the next section.

A Short History of Chaos Theory

The word chaos *traditionally denotes a formless void that is pregnant with forthcoming order. Now we see that <u>disorder in an individual or a society can precede the emergence of new structure</u> instead of leading inevitably to mere anarchy in accordance with the laws of entropy.*

—Walter J. Freeman[8]

From Ptolemy to Poincaré

The first men and women who stared upward at the night sky must have wondered about those points of lights. Surely they felt themselves at the center of the universe; everything else was "out there." It would hardly occur to them to think otherwise. In the second century AD, the Greek astronomer Ptolemy made that feeling explicit, constructing a model of the universe in which a series of clear, perfectly formed, nesting spheres surrounded the earth. The sun, the planets, and the stars rested on those spheres. Since astronomical observations are critical for agriculture, a great deal was already known about the actual positions and movements of the heavenly bodies. But observations had to fit theory, not the other way around. Since calculations based on Ptolemy's perfect spheres did not fit those observations, more and more complex rationalizations had to be made to preserve earth's central position.

Early in the sixteenth century, Copernicus had the brilliant realization that perhaps the earth was not central but was, in fact, moving around the sun. His view seemed sacrilegious to sixteenth-century churchmen, who were convinced that God had created the world and everything in it in six days. From Creation on, in their view, the world had been static and unchanging, apart from a few known exceptions, such as the Flood, that were recorded in the Bible. For them and for most educated Europeans, Ptolemy's views were merely a scientific explication of what they already knew from the Bible. Knowledge of the world didn't need to come from observation; that knowledge was already contained in the Bible. Eventually, though, Copernicus' view won out. But calculations about the positions and movements of the planets still remained less accurate than desired, in large part because it was still assumed that planets moved in circular orbits. True accuracy required the elliptical orbits later specified by Newton's laws of motion.

Newton, using his new insights, was able to completely solve what mathematicians and astronomers call the "two-body problem." In a universe consisting of only two bodies, say the sun and the earth, Newton could predict exactly the movement of those two bodies. Another century passed, and French mathematician and astronomer Pierre-Simon Laplace, in his *Mécanique Céleste* (*Celestial Mechanics*), attempted the "*n*-body problem": describing the movements of all the planets in the solar system. To a great extent, he succeeded. But there were anomalies that didn't always fit the calculations. Still another century was to pass before the problem led to the beginnings of chaos theory.

In 1887, to celebrate the sixtieth birthday of King Oscar of Sweden and Norway, a prize was offered for solving the *n*-body problem. The complete solution proved beyond the power of any mathematician of the time, but the great mathematician Henri Poincaré won the prize in 1899 for his essay on an important piece of the puzzle: the three-body problem, that is, a complete description of the movement of, for example, the earth, sun, and moon. Just as the essay was being prepared for publication in the journal *Acta Mathematica*, Poincaré realized that it contained a deep and critical error. In correcting this error, Poincaré was able to prove that the complete movement of even three bodies was inherently unpredictable. This discovery shook him so badly that he declared, "These things are so bizarre that I cannot bear to contemplate them." Without realizing it, Poincaré had discovered mathematical chaos in the movement of the planets. As with so many seminal discoveries, it was too early for the implications to be fully understood. A new tool was needed: the computer. With it, chaos descended to the earth.

The Computer Changes Everything

The world of mathematics is traditionally a timeless one, in which equations have no future or past. With Darwin's discovery of evolution by natural selection, however, scientists realized that they lived in a world in which time could no longer be ignored. Once the "arrow of time" moves forward, it cannot be reversed. The problem was that scientists lacked the mathematical tools to deal with the arrow of time. Before computers, the only mathematical tool for dealing with change over time was calculus. But calculus is itself composed of equations that can be calculated either forward or backward. If you differentiate an equation for distance, you get velocity. Differentiate again and you get acceleration. Conversely, though, you can equally well start with acceleration and integrate to get first the equation for velocity, then for distance. Thus, calculus by itself cannot capture the one-way nature of time.

With the development of the modern digital computer, a new mathematical world opened up for science. Even the primitive early computers were amazing: not only could they calculate complex equations much faster than any human being, they also could create new types of equations in which the result of each calculation was fed back into the equation over and over, many millions of times (and now billions and even trillions). Now, rather than having to calculate a final outcome directly, scientists could mathematically model a natural phenomenon (such as the weather or fluid dynamics) that changed over time. This powerful new method allowed scientists to cause a model of a natural phenomenon to "evolve" in much the way it would evolve in nature.

Another factor also proved crucial: scientists could now *see* the results changing. In our short history we've now reached the early 1960s. Edward Lorenz, a meteorologist at the Massachusetts Institute of Technology, had programmed a simple model of the weather. Numbers representing initial weather conditions were put into the program, which then calculated what the weather would be after some interval of time. These results were fed back as initial conditions for the next run, and so on. By using this technique, the computer could predict weather conditions over an extended period of time. (It is important to stress, however, that this was a very simple early model, hardly sufficient to deal with all the variables of the weather.) All this was happening long before computers could present true graphics, but programmers used clever tricks to make images out of strings of letters.* Lorenz used a similar technique to create a continuous paper line graph of the output of his model, the numbers describing weather conditions. The line would rise or fall in ways that looked like the movement of the winds or other meteorological phenomena over months or even years.

Because those early computers were very slow, sometimes a run took several days and had to be stopped and restarted. One day Lorenz came into the lab intending to continue the run from the day before. To make sure the results were continuous, he entered the initial positions from the middle of the previous day and went off to some other task. He expected that the computer would reproduce results identical to those from the previous day and then continue on from that point. When he returned to look at the printout, he was shocked to find that the graph looked nothing like the previous day's printout. Initially he thought he had made a mistake, but when he checked the numeric input, he couldn't find any problems. Eventually he realized that the only difference between the two runs was that the computer handled calculations using six decimal places of accuracy, while the printout of numbers, the numbers he had entered the next day, only went to three decimal places. With traditional "static" equations, such a difference would have imperceptible consequences. But since the results of each calculation were fed back as input for the next calculation, over many iterations those tiny differences could grow until they produced a markedly different result. As mentioned in the introduction, this situation has come to be called sensitive dependence on initial conditions or, in layman's terms, the butterfly effect.

Like any good scientist, Lorenz went on to study this puzzling phenomenon in a variety of ways involving not only the weather but convection currents in general. Finally, in his words: *"I realized that any physical system that behaved nonperiodically would be unpredictable."*[9] Thus was chaos theory born.[10]

Computers have improved by orders of magnitude since Lorenz did his initial work, and the ability to see models of nature has become indispensable

---

* People who remember this era of computers may recall the great fun programmers had with printing these pictures; Snoopy was a favorite.

for scientists. Lorenz had only a simple paper-tape graph, but even that was a breakthrough. Scientists can now see the results of their mathematical models as a picture in color and three dimensions on a computer screen: they can examine any portion of the picture at any depth, rotate the results, move forward or backwards in time, and so on. In other words, scientists can see nature—albeit still somewhat simplified—on a computer screen. Because of this visual aspect, results can be easily shared and understood not only by fellow experts in the field but also by scientists from other disciplines and even nonscientists. This increased level of communication has changed the nature of science dramatically.

These improvements in technology have only reinforced Lorenz's discovery that with *complex systems* (like human beings and heartbeats and stock markets and most everything else in the world of sufficient complexity to be of interest), it is impossible to fully predict outcomes. It's true that in most situations, the outcome is usually close enough to what was predicted by the normal scientific laws that we consider that the laws hold. But sometimes, and no one can define how often "sometimes" is, the results are totally different from what was predicted. Chaos theorists have examined closely the types of situations in which results begin diverging widely and eventually end up in chaos. They have also shown that the feedback that makes unexpected change possible is also what keeps complex systems intact in a changing world. The human body, for example, is constantly feeding information about itself back into itself, so that we can grow from childhood to adulthood yet still retain our identity, even if every single molecule of our body changes over that time. What is true for the body is no less true for the psyche. Our thoughts and feelings and actions are constantly fed back into our memory and affect our future thoughts and feelings and actions. Normally we continue to develop along an existing path that is largely predictable from our past. But just as a tiny change in Edward Lorenz's data caused his graphs suddenly to look very different, tiny changes in our lives can lead to new directions that could never have been predicted from what came before.

We'll discuss all of this in more detail later in the book. But for now, it's enough to realize that, in nature, often the only way to find out the final result is to wait and see what happens.

THE OLD IS NEW

Let's retrace our steps a moment before heading into the details of the alchemical principles and their modern equivalents. In this chapter, we saw how alchemy emerged in the West at roughly the same time as Christianity. It went underground, largely in the Arab countries, and then moved back into the Western world after the Arabs conquered Spain. From there it moved slowly into Europe, flourished, and then largely died. Newton, in the seventeenth century, could be seen as the pivot point, not only as the beginning of a new order, but also as the last of the great alchemists.

Science replaced alchemy and for several centuries seemed to have no limits; everything in nature was predictable. Late in the nineteenth century, however, Poincaré discovered that the complete movement of even three heavenly bodies, such as the earth, moon, and sun, was unpredictable. And then with Lorenz's discovery of chaos theory, the way was reopened for Nature (not merely "nature") to reemerge. Not surprisingly, alchemy's insights emerged again, though with a vastly different vocabulary. And, because a millennium had passed since the beginnings of alchemy, the new science brings a more profound understanding to some (though only some) of the age-old issues. Not surprisingly, those insights, old and new, also have profound implications for how the process of self-transformation occurs in each of our lives, as we will see in later chapters.

~The Story of Alchemy and Chaos Theory~

2

As Above, So Below

The human on earth is a mortal god but that god in heaven is an immortal human. Through these two, then, cosmos and human, all things exist, but they all exist by action of the one.

—*Corpus Hermeticum* X:25

The idea that the *macrocosm* (the universe or God) and the *microcosm* (the physical world, a human being) are inherently connected is the first crucial element of alchemy that we will study in this chapter. The equivalent understanding in chaos theory is that the *global* and the *local* are inextricably mixed, so that each affects the other. In particular, complex systems are self-similar at any dimensionality. Let us begin our journey with Hermes Trismegistus and the Emerald Tablet.

ALCHEMY

The mysteries of the Great and the Little World are distinguished only by the form in which they manifest themselves; for they are only one thing, one being.

—Paracelsus[1]

Hermes Trismegistus and the Emerald Tablet

Perhaps the single most important belief of alchemy is contained in the phrase "as above, so below," which first appeared in the opening lines of the fabled text called the Emerald Tablet, also known as the Smaragdine Table or the Tabula Smaragdin. Many consider that the entire alchemical opus is contained within the fourteen lines of the Emerald Tablet, which has been translated dozens of times over the years. The full fourteen lines of Newton's version, with the archaisms of the seventeenth-century spelling modernized, appear below. According to legend, this text was literally written on a tablet of emerald (though the Greek phrase could simply mean "green rock"), which was discovered in a cave, clutched in the hands of the corpse of the legendary Egyptian figure Hermes Trismegistus (i.e., "thrice greatest Hermes").

The Emerald Tablet

1. Tis true without lying, certain & most true.

2. That which is below is like that which is above & that which is above is like that which is below to do ye miracles of one only thing.

3. And as all things have been & arose from one by the mediation of one: so all things have their birth from this one thing by adaptation.

4. The Sun is its father, the moon its mother.

5. The wind hath carried it in its belly, the earth its nurse.

6. The father of all perfection in the whole world is here.

7. Its force or power is entire if it be converted into earth.

7a. Separate the earth from the fire, the subtle from the gross sweetly with great industry.

8. It ascends from the earth to the heaven & again it descends to the earth and receives the force of things superior & inferior.

9. By this means you shall have the glory of the whole world & thereby all obscurity shall fly from you.

10. Its force is above all force. For it vanquishes every subtle thing & penetrates every solid thing.

11. So was the world created.

12. From this are & do come admirable adaptations whereof the means is here in this.

13. Hence I am called Hermes Trismegistus, having the three parts of the philosophy of the whole world.

14. That which I have said of the operation of the Sun is accomplished & ended.

—translated from the Latin by Isaac Newton[2]

Hermes Trismegistus was identified initially with the Greek god Hermes, or with his Egyptian counterpart, Thoth; still later the Latin name Mercurius came into use interchangeably with the other names. Some versions of the legend claimed Hermes Trismegistus was the first and greatest of three men named Hermes. This first Hermes was the grandson of Adam and wrote widely about science and mathematics; among his many writings was the Emerald Tablet. Some claimed that Noah took the tablet with him on the Ark during the Flood and later preserved it in a cave where it was discovered by Sarah, the wife of Abraham. Another version claimed that the tablet was discovered by Alexander the Great in the fourth century BC. In still another version, it was the neo-Pythagorean philosopher Apollonius of Tyana (first century AD), who discovered the tablet and recorded it in one of his books, from which it passed on to other books in other cultures, including Greece, Syria, and the Islamic alchemists, and from them eventually in Latin translations to European alchemists.[3]

Perhaps the most widespread version was simply that there had existed a series of legendary figures, each of whom transmitted hidden wisdom to successive generations. In this respect, Italian philosopher and astrologer Marsilio Ficino's medieval translations of Plato and some of the Hermetica* influenced many later generations of scholars. In the preface to *A Book on the Power and Wisdom of God, Whose Title is Pimander*, Ficino traced

---

* The *Hermetica* is a loose term for all the literature that was attributed to Hermes Trismegistus. A collection of the suriving texts was published in the Renaissance as the *Corpus Hermeticum*.

a succession that began with Mercurius, then passed on through his grandson Mercurius Trismegistus to Orpheus, Pythagoras, and Philolaus, and culminated in Plato.[4]

The hermetic documents had both occult and scholarly appeal. Much of the scholarship ignored the occult material, while those in the occult tradition had less interest in the purely philosophical material. This divergence led to problems with some of the early records of the works, from which the magical material was often excised. However, scholarship advanced and eventually attempted to restore this aspect to the hermetic documents. For some time, it was generally accepted that the hermetic documents originated in Egypt, though timelines could vary widely, depending on the scholar. However, this origin was seemingly discredited by textual analysis early in the twentieth century, which purported to show that the Egyptian origin was highly unlikely. Instead, other places of origin were suggested, varying from Syria to China. But with the discovery of hermetic documents among the Nag Hammadi codices in the period after World War II, the origin of these ideas was again placed as least as far as the period when Greek and Egyptian culture intertwined in Egypt. In fact, the earliest known attribution of the phrase "thrice greatest" to Thoth or Hermes was discovered on an Egyptian potsherd written early in the third century BC by a man who had named himself Hor, after the god Horus. In this document he referred to "the soul of Thoth, the three times great."[5]

The Emerald Tablet itself appears to be a later addition to the Hermetica; the earliest documented source for the tablet is an eighth-century pseudo-Aristotelian Arabic text, which was translated into Latin in both the twelfth and thirteenth centuries.[6] It is likely, however, that it evolved from earlier documents and may well have its origin in more primitive versions that go back to the same Greco-Egyptian period as the rest of the Hermetica.

The Soul in Greek Thought

Jungian analyst Marie-Louise von Franz remarked that alchemy came into existence "when the thought models of the Greek philosophy met with the experimental practices of the Egyptian traditions."[7] We also see this mix of Greek and Egyptian ideas in the concept of reincarnation and the soul, which only slowly evolved into the more explicit alchemical concept of "as above, so below." We are going to look at that development, first with the ancient Greeks, then with the Gnostics in the early part of the Christian era, then with Paracelsus at the peak of alchemy's history in the sixteenth century.

In the second volume of his *Histories*, the Greek historian Herodotus (often called the "father of history") wrote in the fifth century BC that "the Egyptians were also the first to claim that the human soul was immortal, and that each time the body dies the soul enters another creature just as it is being born."[8] This belief had become widely influential in Greek thought through the teachings of Pythagoras a century earlier. Though we know Pythagoras and his teachings only through secondary sources, many of them fragmentary, we can make some educated guesses as to his views. One early and influential source is *The Life of Pythagoras*, which was contained in *Lives of the Eminent Philosophers*, written by Diogenes Laertius in the third century. Laertius says that Pythagoras taught that "there is a relationship between men and the Gods, because men partake of the divine principle, on which count, therefore, God exercises his providence for our advantage."[9] This quote highlights two key points. First, human beings possess a divine principle that connects us with God (or the gods). This divine principle, the soul, is thus an explicit example of "as above, so below." Second, God continues to have an effect on our lives and isn't simply an absentee landlord. Here the "above" acts upon the "below," rather than the two simply being united at the creation of human beings.

Laertius (speaking for Pythagoras) makes a comparison with the sun, whose rays penetrate through the air, the water, and the earth, its heat giving life to all things. Because plants depend on this principle of heat as much as animals do, he concludes that plants are living things. He does not, however, consider that all living things have a soul. "The soul is something different from life. It is immortal, because of the immortality from which it was torn."[10]

The Pythagorean soul has three parts: intelligence and reason (which both come from the brain) and passion (which comes from the heart).

The soul thus partakes of both heart and brain. It is man's task to find the harmony among these three parts. This harmony comes both from God and from man's own choices. This idea of finding a harmony between man as simply a living being, subject to mortality, and man's soul, which is immortal, is an essential part of the Pythagorean ideal, an ideal not necessarily shared by later thinkers (as we will see).

By *harmony*, the Pythagoreans weren't referring to some vague ideal; they meant that everything in the universe fits together in a rational fashion, determined by numeric relationships. More than any other such group, before or since, the Pythagoreans regarded *number* as the unifying principle inherent in and between all things. They were the first to discover that the musical intervals were all ratios of the simple counting numbers. The harmony of music was an example in the world "below" of the *harmony of the spheres* (their term for an entire universe filled with planets and stars)— the world "above." A famous story (perhaps apocryphal) shows how vital this principle was to the Pythagoreans: when one of their followers discovered that the square root of two could not be expressed as the ratio of any two counting numbers (i.e., that it is "irrational"), he was drowned and his discovery hushed up.

In the Pythagorean view, the soul's desire was to return to that eternal harmony from which it had emerged; the philosopher's goal was to help the soul find its way back to the divine harmony through a series of stages: first, an ethical purification of the soul; second, contemplation of the universal harmony in nature; third, a mystical union with God. Accordingly, unlike later groups we will discuss, the Pythagoreans did not believe the physical world in general, and our bodies in particular, to be an evil that needed to be transcended. Because they believed in a universal harmony that ran though all things, the world and the body were part of that harmony. Though the soul was eternal, it existed within the world.[11]

By the time of Plato in the fourth century BC, the Pythagorean creation myth had modified. There was still an ultimate God—the One—who was the source of all, but the work of creation was left to the demiurge (i.e., divine craftsman). In the *Timaeus*, Plato presents an elaborate description of the stages of creation of the universe, which he sees as ordered and perfect, a representation of the perfection of its creator. Although, like Pythagoras, he sees a harmony in all, this perfection could only be a product of intellectual reason. Humanity's task is to regard the world through our intellect and through this process come closer to grasping the divine intellect that created it. Therefore, though the soul was still regarded as having three parts, the intelligence, reason, and passion of Pythagoras had evolved into reason, emotion, and appetite. Both emotion and appetite were viewed as lower passions to be transcended. The soul, rather than seeking the harmony of all three, was now governed only by reason. Plato still makes a connection between the divinity above and humanity below, but only through intellectual reason. How far can it be from that place to Descartes' declaration, "I think, therefore I am"?

Aristotle offers another fourth-century view of the soul: neither that of Pythagoras nor Plato, but one perhaps closer to a modern scientific view, if science acknowledged a soul. Whereas Pythagoras believed that not all living things had souls, Aristotle viewed soul as another word for that which emerged when life existed within a body; in other words, soul was an epiphenomenon. Rather than sharply demarcating plants and animals from humans, with only the latter possessing an immortal soul, he considered that there existed a progressive chain of souls, with the souls of animals above those of plants, and human souls, because of human reason, above those of animals. But all living creatures were mortal and the soul was inconceivable apart from a living body. Hence, for Aristotle, there is no longer anything that fits the pattern of "as above, so below."

Gnostic Thought

We've considered these three Greek thinkers—Pythagoras, Plato, and Aristotle—because their views, transformed over time, were to influence all later thinkers. For example, the Gnostic Christians, who flourished in the first centuries of the Christian era, believed that we could best follow Christ's example not only by living ethically, but also by trying, like Christ, to experience God within ourselves. The Gnostic ideal was for direct religious experience, mystical experience, *gnosis* (divine knowledge).

We, too, could experience the numinous! Though the Gnostic Christians comprised diverse sects that varied widely in their beliefs, many Gnostic writers combined Christianity with Greek thought, largely through what they knew of the works of "the ancients," that is, Plato, Aristotle, and Pythagoras, whose work they conflated into a single set of beliefs, no matter how poorly the individual pieces fit together. Like Plato, they believed that the universe was not a "creation" of the ultimate God, but instead an emanation from a lesser divinity, a demiurge. The Gnostics had an elaborate model of the stages through which that emanation took place. But whereas the demiurge was, in Plato's view, a perfect architect, to many of the Gnostics the demiurge was the source of the imperfection and evil of our world. Because of this belief that the world had been corrupted in the very process of creation, the disparagement of the body reached its peak in some Gnostic sects. The body was considered an evil that needed to be transcended in order to retrace the steps leading back to the divine.

However, that picture of Gnosticism may not tell the whole story. A modern Gnostic bishop and scholar, Stephan Hoeller, has combined Gnostic beliefs with Jungian depth psychology in his lectures and books. Hoeller questions the interpretation that Gnostics considered the physical world and the human body to be evil. The Gnostics were still at a prepsychological stage of development, but in their symbolic teachings, Hoeller argues, they were struggling to express the idea that it is our lack of consciousness that creates the evils of the world:

> It is *not* the physical world with its earth and trees, but the *system* (in Greek *kosmos*) created by unconsciousness that is evil, or at least relatively so. It is *not* an ethereal heaven, but individuated consciousness that the pneumatic [i.e., filled with spirit, from the Greek *pneuma*] Gnostic attains to when the limitations of unconsciousness are overcome by Gnosis. It is *not* sexuality that is evil, but the psyche's bondage to blind instinctuality with its accompanying unconsciousness. It is *not* life that is rejected, but a life of brutish unconsciousness, which is the cause of most of humanity's afflictions. The Demiurge is *none other* than the human ego, alienated from

its deeper psychic background (the Pleroma): arrogant, one-sided, and having rejected the wisdom of the Feminine.[12]

Jung regarded the Gnostics as prepsychological forerunners to his own discoveries about the psyche. They were trying to reconcile the perfection of the divine (the "above") with the imperfection that they experienced (the "below").

Paracelsus

In the previous chapter, we briefly traced the twisted path that alchemy took after the time of the Gnostics and saw that it reached its peak in the fifteenth and sixteenth centuries. We are now going to jump forward to a man whose strong belief in the alchemical model changed medicine: sixteenth-century physician Philippus Aureolus Bombast von Hohenheim, more commonly known as Theophrastus Paracelsus, or simply Paracelsus. Like Jung, Paracelsus was Swiss, accordingly blessed (or cursed) with, in Jung's words, "that characteristically Swiss obstinacy, doggedness, stolidity, and innate pride that have been interpreted in various ways—favorably as self-reliance, unfavorably as dour pigheadedness."[13]

Paracelsus was born the illegitimate son of a wandering doctor who settled in the small Swiss town of Einsiedeln. Though he was to become someone who challenged the existing medical establishment and arrived at new ways of viewing the relationship between disease and health, as a young man, he was hardly physically prepossessing, with "a stature of a mere five feet, an unhealthy appearance, an upper lip that was too short and did not quite cover his teeth . . . and, so it seems, a pelvis that struck everybody by its femininity."[14] Despite that appearance, or perhaps because of it, he strutted around life with an arrogance that earned him many enemies, especially among his fellow physicians, whose methods he reviled. Like the heroic figure he thought himself to be, he carried a sword that was too big for his body. In its pommel were the laudanum (i.e., tincture of opium) pills that were a mainstay of his medical treatments.

He was a physician, an alchemist, an astrologer, an occultist, and one of the most prolific authors of the Renaissance. While still in his teens, he studied medicine at the University of Basel. Always on the move, he then went first to Vienna and later gained his doctorate from the University of Ferrara in Italy. Unsatisfied by the methods he learned at the Western universities, he continued his traveling ways, roaming through Egypt, Arabia, the Near East, Constantinople, Lisbon, Spain, and England, always looking for newer methods, methods that fit in with his holistic view of reality.[15] "On his long journeys Paracelsus gathered a rich harvest of experience, not scorning even the grimiest sources, for he was a "pragmatist and empiricist without parallel."[16]

The Renaissance was a time when thinkers turned their eyes to the physical world around them and began to observe and measure it carefully in ways that few had done earlier. They looked both above and below: outward toward the heavens and down to the earth they lived upon; they even looked for the first time inside the human body. For example, barely two years after Paracelsus' death, the year 1543 brought publication of both Copernicus' *Concerning the Revolution of the Heavenly Bodies* (which established modern astronomy) and Andreas Vesalius' *Concerning the Structure of the Human Body* (which established modern human anatomy).

Paracelsus was interested less in either of the two worlds than in the hermetic doctrine that the two were necessarily connected. In Paracelsus' words: "Heaven is man, and man is heaven, and all men together are one heaven, and heaven is nothing but one man."[17] This lovely phrase means not only "as above, so below," but also "as below, so above." With this idea of mutual influence, Paracelsus comes closer to the view of chaos theory than any previous thinker.

Like most physicians of his day, Paracelsus was a practicing astrologer, but his view of what that meant was more complex than a simple belief in the influence of the heavens upon man and thus the need to look for propitious times for treatments. If we follow his belief, each of us is composed of an earthly part and a heavenly part, or, as he said, "Man is the child of two fathers—one father is the earth, the other is heaven . . . From the earth he receives the material body, from heaven his character."[18] Thus our characters are, as all believers in astrology argue, determined at the moment of birth by the total form of the heavens. That connection also means, if we adopt his view, that each of us carries a particular heaven with us at all times. Furthermore, the heavens above are composed of all these individual heavens. Paracelsus insisted that "the stars must obey man and be subject to him, and not he to the stars."[19] Since each of us carries a portion of heaven determined by our birth, we control the heavens above as we control our own lives. "It is not true that the firmament exerts a compelling action upon man; on the contrary man himself acts upon the world more than he is influenced by it."[20]

When Paracelsus returned to Europe, his medical treatments went completely against the grain of most of his colleagues. Unlike them, he drew on alchemical ideas in his healing methods. For example, the prevailing treatment of the time for wounds was to cauterize them with boiling oil; if a wound on an arm or leg was serious, the arm or leg was allowed to become gangrenous, then amputated. With his belief in the harmony of nature, so similar to that of Pythagoras, Paracelsus trusted in the body's ability to heal itself if given the proper chance. Accordingly, instead of cauterizing the wounds or allowing them to become gangrenous, he would drain the wounds to prevent infection and then let the body do the healing. "This attack on physicians . . . started a struggle which changed medicine for ever [sic]. Together with the invention of printing, this movement drove the distribution of texts and the exchange of recipes."[21]

Though it isn't obvious, this healing approach flowed again out of his belief in the alchemical model of "heaven above, heaven below," or, in the case of medical treatments, that "everything that is within can be known by what is without."[22] Just as the heavens determine our character and the earth our physical being, there is a wholeness to our body and character that is reflected at all levels. With a man or woman, to see this reflection one could look to his or her extremities, the hands and feet; or to the face and head; or to the shape of the body; or to the gestures and manners. All would tell about the inner nature. (As we will see later in this chapter, this quality of part-reveals-whole is exactly what chaos theory means when reality is described as being "fractal.")

In a word, Paracelsus practiced *chiromancy*, though that word meant far more to him than its current, impoverished definition of "palm reading." For Paracelsus, chiromancy was a general principle that permeated all reality: "From the external [the physician] sees the internal. Only external things give knowledge of the internal; without them, no internal thing may be known."[23] He proceeded not only from the external of the patient, but also from the external in nature to the internal in a human being. For example, he said that the physician had to look to how copper was made in order to understand leprosy, to rust on iron to understand ulcerations. The central concept was that "like cures like." This breakthrough concept led physicians for the first time to use chemical treatments for diseases. As such it is the foundation for all modern medicine. In his treatments he used arsenic, mercury, sulfur, iron, copper sulfate, and other metals. His idea of like curing like is also the basis for the more controversial modern method of "cell therapy," in which cells are taken from an organ of a person's body, allowed to multiply in a laboratory environment, then injected back into the patient's body to cure the damaged organ. Other modern variants on "like cures like" include blood transfusions, bone marrow transfusions, and stem-cell therapies.

Paracelsus also believed that these methods, powerful as they were, could only be effective if the physician approached the patients with compassion and even love, because it was love that could bridge the seemingly inseparable distances between human beings: "First of all it is very necessary to tell of the compassion that must be innate in a physician . . . Where there is no love, there is no art . . . The practice of this art lies in the heart: if your heart is false, the physician within you will be false."[24]

CHAOS THEORY: FRACTALS

Causality is considered multilevel and multideterminate. Any level or domain of observation or theory may communicate with others without necessarily going through a linear causal chain.

—Frederick David Abraham[25]

Previously we encountered Paracelsus' saying that "Heaven is man, and man is heaven, and all men together are one heaven, and heaven is nothing but one man."[26] Compare those words with the above quote from chaos theorist Frederick Abraham. While Paracelsus' expression is lovelier, Abraham's is more explicit: the above can affect the below, or equally the below affect the above, without any intermediate chain of connections. We see examples of this kind of direct link in the phenomenon of fractals.

The term *fractal* was invented by Benoit Mandelbrot, who created the whole field of fractal mathematics. It comes from the Latin adjective *fractus*; the related verb form, *frangere*, means "to break apart" or "to create irregular fragments." In fractal mathematics, the natural world is presented not as regular and continuous in the familiar way, but as irregular and fraught with discontinuities, a nature composed of fragments. But surprisingly, a new order comes into view when we look at nature as fragmented: the fragments combine over and over to make the wholes. The following are two of many definitions of *fractal*:

- A complex geometric figure whose small-scale and large-scale structures resemble one another.

- A mathematically generated pattern that is reproducible at any magnification or reduction.

The most famous traditional attempt to portray these qualities is the *Taijitu*, the classic yin-yang symbol (figure 2.1). This symbol represents the unity of yin and yang, the two polarities of energy in Chinese thought, in which each contains the other. The small dots inside each half portray this containment.

Figure 2.1. Yin-yang symbol.

Chapter Two

But, by implication, there is no end to this process: the yin within the yang in turn contains both yin and yang, and the process continues endlessly.

To put it in a single word, fractals are *self-similar*; that is, they look the same no matter where you look within the fractal. Mathematicians had discovered many such unusual geometric figures that predated Mandelbrot's discovery of fractals. For example, in a 1904 paper, the Swedish mathematician Helge von Koch presented what has come to be known as the Koch snowflake. To picture this, take an equilateral triangle (i.e., each side is the same length); divide each side into thirds and on the middle third build another equilateral triangle. Continue this process with those triangles, and with all subsequent triangles. Figure 2.2 shows this process progressing through three stages; figure 2.3 shows the result after eight stages.

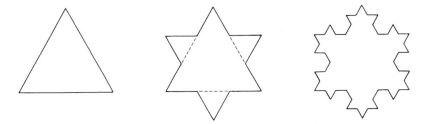

Figure 2.2. Koch snowflake, stages 1–3.

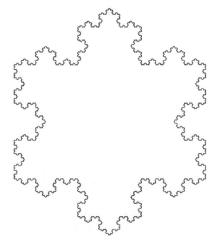

Figure 2.3. Koch snowflake, stage 8.

A closely related figure that reveals self-similarity even more strongly is the Sierpiński triangle, described by mathematician Wacław Sierpiński in 1916. In this case, take another equilateral triangle, but this time, divide it into four equilateral triangles and remove the middle one. Continue this process with all the triangles that emerge (figure 2.4). Or instead of a triangle, take a square, divide it into smaller squares, and remove the middle ones (figure 2.5). Again the process continues. The process can be used just as readily on three-dimensional objects or even higher dimensional objects, though of course we can no longer see what those look like. The most famous of the three-dimensional objects is the Sierpiński cube (figure 2.6).

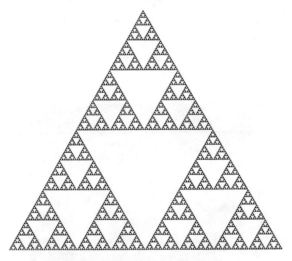

Figure 2.4. Sierpiński triangle.

Until Mandelbrot, however, these strange figures were considered to be anomalous or even "pathological." The history of mathematics is filled with examples in which the new is dismissed as pathological in one way or another. Recall the follower of Pythagoras who was drowned for his discovery that the square root of two was *irrational*. (Note the word *irrational* for such numbers.) *Negative* numbers, that is, numbers less than zero, suffered the same fate. When, in the sixteenth century, mathematicians increasingly found solutions of equations that involved what was then

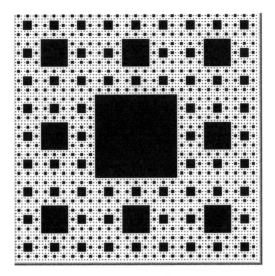

Figure 2.5. Sierpiński square.

Figure 2.6. Sierpiński cube.

considered an impossibility—the square root of a negative number—they were forced to make use of such monsters, but solaced themselves by calling them *imaginary*.

Mandelbrot introduced the concept of fractals to the scientific community in a wildly iconoclastic three-page paper that somehow slipped into the illustrious (and usually staid) pages of *Science* in 1967; its title was "How Long is the Coast of Britain?"[27] This paper has become known not only to mathematicians, but also to the general public, though usually for the wrong reason. The article title would lead one to think the issue is measurement. Reference books do often give figures for the length of the coastline of various countries. But it's self-evident that the length depends on the measuring device. If a ruler is used instead of a yardstick, the coastline will be much longer, because the ruler can measure smaller differences in its shape. If we let the unit of measure get smaller and smaller, ultimately the length of any coast will be infinite. That's what most people think Mandelbrot's paper was about.

Actually he had discovered something quite different. He had come across a 1961 paper by Lewis Fry Richardson, to whom Mandelbrot later referred as "a great scientist whose originality mixed with eccentricity."[28] Richardson had found that the approximate length of various actual coastlines could be calculated by a simple formula into which you plugged the length of measurement you were using. Of more interest for Mandelbrot, the formula included a variable D that varied only by coastline. There was one value of D for the coast of Spain, another for Britain, and so forth. This characteristic was exactly what Mandelbrot meant by *fractal* (though he hadn't come up with the word yet). Mandelbrot's breakthrough was to recognize that the variable D was actually a dimension, even though it wasn't a whole number. In other words, he proposed that, in addition to the single dimension of a straight line, the two dimensions of figures on a plane, the three dimensions of solid objects, and the hard-to-visualize integer dimensions beyond that, there could be fractional dimensions. For example, in the paper, he calculated that the dimension of the west coast of Britain was approximately 1.25.

We needn't be concerned with the math here. What is significant is that the math produced figures that were self-similar no matter what level one looked at. The key to that discovery was computers. By 1973, Mandelbrot was working for IBM as a fellow at the Thomas J. Watson Research Center, where he was surrounded by high-speed computers. It was better than Disneyland! He worked out formulas that, when fed back into themselves over and over (as with everything else in chaos theory), produced calculated coastlines that actually looked like real coastlines.

> We rigged up a very clumsy plotter to produce artificial coastlines . . . Sometimes we had to sit up all night with plotters. But when the first coastline finally came out, we were all amazed. It looked just like New Zealand! Here was an elongated island, there a squarish one, and, off to one side, two specks resembling Bounty Island . . . Seeing them had an electrifying effect on everyone . . . Now after seeing the coastline pictures, everyone agreed with me that fractals were a part of the stuff of nature.[29]

With that exciting result, the sky was the limit, and Mandelbrot went on to generate clouds and trees and rivers and almost anything else imaginable in nature. The implication was that, since he could generate something that looked remarkably like a natural phenomenon by building it up out of little self-similar pieces, then nature itself might use the same technique. Nature might be fractal. And if nature is fractal, our knowledge of it is also necessarily fractal. In Isaac Asimov's words: "I believe that scientific knowledge has fractal properties, that no matter how much we learn, whatever is left, however small it may seem, is just as infinitely complex as the whole was to start with. That, I think, is the secret of the Universe."[30]

The most famous of all fractal creations is the Mandelbrot set, which is the most complex mathematical object in existence. As with all the earlier fractals, it's generated from a very simple formula[31] with the results fed back over and over again. It's normally generated in color to highlight distinctions, but a beautiful black-and-white version follows. The shadings in color between black and white were generated by the average differences between iterations.

Imagine that you had an enormously powerful microscope that you could use to look at any part of this figure. What you'd see through the microscope would look remarkably like the whole picture you're seeing now. What makes this object more interesting than the fractal objects

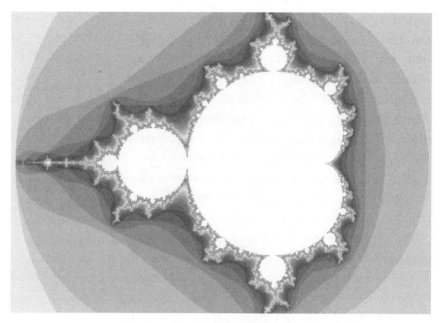

Figure 2.7. The Mandelbrot set.

you've seen earlier in this chapter is that you would find creative differences between the original figure and its copies at each deeper level. These approximations to the original look very similar, but each has variations of its own, as if some celestial artist kept working with it at every level.

The new insight that chaos theory and fractals give on the ancient idea of "as above, so below" is that beautiful variations on a theme may emerge without us having any way of predicting what they will be.

LESSONS FOR SELF-TRANSFORMATION

Alchemy and chaos theory offer different but complementary insights into the importance of the concept of "as above, so below" in the process of self-transformation. This central concept evolved among the Greek thinkers as an attempt to explain how humanity, with all its limitations, could be related to some higher power. At its extreme, these thinkers were trying to answer how something physical could emerge out of the divine. What is glorious in all their approaches is simply the idea that we all contain the possibility for greatness of spirit, a spark of divinity. Most spiritual traditions settle on one or another of the explanations we saw earlier. Many, like Plato (and the early Christians, and many of the Gnostics), regard the physical and the spiritual as separate and distinct. This position has often led to a denigration of the body and its needs as at best a necessary nuisance; at worst, sinful. Whole traditions are based on advancing past the body and its needs toward an ever more ethereal spiritual goal. I'm reminded of bad science-fiction movies, in which aliens (supposedly more advanced than we are) are always portrayed with enormous heads for thinking and bodies atrophied to the point where they can hardly walk.

Though Pythagoras was among the first to deal with the idea of "as above, so below," his belief system can still teach us a lot, in that he believed in a harmony between body and spirit, just as there was a harmony of all in the universe. We may advance in spirituality, but we do so while living in a physical body. Perhaps the wisest way to view these ancient thoughts as models of transformation is to follow Stephan Hoeller's interpretation of Gnostic thought, which we discussed earlier: "It is . . . the *system* . . . created by unconsciousness that is evil, or at least relatively so . . . It is *not* life that is rejected, but a life of brutish unconsciousness, which is the cause of most of humanity's afflictions."[32]

Paracelsus gave us several important additional insights. Like the ancients, he believed that the astrological state of the heavens helped determine our individual personalities. But he took that belief a bit further by adding the insight that each of us therefore carries our own heaven with us throughout our lives: as we grow and change, so does our heaven. Thus, each of us has an effect on the totality of all. Not only are we all affected by the godhead, we also affect it! Here is how psychiatrist R. D. Laing put it in his strange and beautiful book, *Knots*:

All in all
Each man in all men
all men in each man

As Above, So Below

All being in each being
Each being in all being
All in each
Each in all.[33]

This was a very deep insight, one that itself evolved over a long period until it found perfect expression. A precursor of it can be traced back at least as far as Lao Tzu. Plato and the Greek poet Xenophanes expressed it in embryonic form. I first encountered this idea while I was in college in an essay by American transcendentalist Ralph Waldo Emerson called "Circles." But perhaps it has found its clearest expression in the memorable phrase of seventeenth-century mathematician and philosopher Blaise Pascal: "Nature is an infinite sphere, the center of which is everywhere, the circumference nowhere." Each person not only contains a spark of divinity, as the early Greeks thought; each is, in addition, and despite the paradox it involves, the center of all that is divine.

Chaos theory provides its own unique insights into the idea of "as above, so below." With the Mandelbrot set and other fractals, we saw the possibility of complexity that was self-similar at all levels. As a psychologist, I know that this is just as true of human behavior, whether as a snapshot at any point in time or as a person transforms over time. Each person's personality is unique and affects everything they do, so that if we look closely enough at a person's behavior in any one situation, we can come close to predicting how that person will think and behave in all situations. In the words of clinical psychologist Dr. Terry Marks-Tarlow:

> People tend to resemble themselves in fundamental ways that are independent of spatial, temporal, or situational scales of observation. When they possess a certain psychological characteristic, they tend to exhibit that characteristic at many, if not all, levels. An aggressive person demonstrates that trait over and over, whether at the verbal level of hogging air space in a conversation, the behavioral level of pushing to the front of a line, or the tactical level of pushing a colleague aside to get a promotion at work.[34]

41

You can also see how, as people change over time, they remain the same essential person. Nineteenth-century British poet William Wordsworth expressed this truth beautifully in his phrase "the child is father of the man."[35] That's not to say self-transformation is impossible; rather, the transformed person is still, in some essential way, contained in the child, as an oak is contained in an acorn. We saw that within the self-similarity of fractals, unexpected creative differences can emerge, yet the larger pattern holds. Aristotle's term for this truth was *entelechy*. Loosely translated it means that the end is contained in the beginning. As we will see in the next chapter, this idea that "one is all" lies at the core of the alchemical model. Too often, people on a spiritual path get confused and think that somehow they should be transformed into someone totally different. But we are each unique, and our possibilities are unique unto each of us. At the end of our journeys in life, we arrive to find the child looking back at us.

Though self-similar at all levels, the Mandelbrot set is also infinitely complex. And "infinitely" is not an exaggeration: there is no limit to how deep one can dive in the Mandelbrot set, and at each level, not only is the whole repeated, but we find differences that occur nowhere else in the total figure. If this infinitely complex mathematical object could be created by the repeated action of a simple formula, think how much more complex a human being is. There is no limit to how deep one can explore within each personality. Even as we change over time, we will always find something that is still uniquely us, but each discovery reveals new beauties that could never be predicted.

Just as Paracelsus looked to the outside to understand the inside, chaos theory now allows us to look at the global picture, the outside, to begin to understand the local, the inside. We may no longer be able to predict with finality the result, but we can see global limits on the possible results. And we can see the types of situations in which no such limits can be determined, where the final results are totally chaotic.

~ As Above, So Below ~

3

Feedback

Feedback has come to mean information about the outcome of any process or activity. No single word seems to have existed in the English language before feedback was introduced in the context of cybernetics, and the analogy filled a gap.

—Steve Heims

All of chaos theory is based on the feedback of the results of a calculation to become the starting point of the next calculation. This process of feedback was what led Lorenz to discover chaos theory. This discovery was made only recently because, without computers, there was no practical way for scientists to model the way the natural world is composed of endless loops of information feeding back upon themselves.

The alchemists, however, had already realized that it was this process of feedback through many stages that begins to separate out potential new structures. The key idea is that a miniscule change caused by an alchemical operation can be magnified many times if the same operation is repeated over and over. In his classic book *Alchemy*, E. J. Holmyard said, "A curious belief held by alchemists was that, even if they had discovered a process that would lead to success, the probabilities were that the substance used would have to be repeatedly subjected to this process—perhaps for hundreds of times—before the glorious end of the work revealed itself. It was a very ancient and primitive belief, for we find it among the Chinese alchemists no less than among later adepts."[1] Perhaps this repetition was neither "curious" nor "primitive" but simply in tune with the natural world.

Chapter Three

ALCHEMY

For nature is a perpetuall circulatory worker, generating fluids
out of solids, and solids out of liquids, fixed things out of volatile,
& volatile out of fixed, subtile out of gross, & gross out of subtile.

—Isaac Newton[2]

The alchemists used the word *opus* to describe the full process needed to produce the philosopher's stone. This process began with the *prima materia*, that is, the first matter, the seed. If, as they believed, the end of the alchemical opus is contained *in potentia* in the *prima materia* that is the beginning point, these repeated operations gradually separate that seed, purify it, and bring it to completion. This happens through a series of repeated stages of *solutio* (dissolving) and *coagulatio* (coagulating, thickening), *separatio* (separating) and *coniunctio* (joining), with another operation, *calcinatio*, to heat the mixture at different points. There were also operations that were even more explicitly related to feedback: the up-and-down movements of the *sublimatio* (sublimating, aerating, rising, making more spiritual), the *mortificatio* (mortifying, falling into matter), and especially the *circulatio* (circulating, continual cycles of rising and falling). The essence of the process was that the alchemical mixture was fed back into itself in complex ways, forming the symbol of the *uroboros*, the snake that swallows its tail.

The Uroboros

The symbol of the uroboros is very ancient indeed (figure 3.1). As early as 4200 BC, the Chinese created jade images of the *zhulong* (literally, "dragon-pig"). This odd creature, a cross between a snake and a pig, wrapped around itself to form a circle. Over time the figure became more graceful and, scholars speculate, evolved into the Chinese dragon, which is regarded as a figure of power and luck.

In the West, the uroboros first appeared in Egypt as early as 1600 BC. It served as a symbol of the eternal cycle of death and resurrection, in which each is inseparable from the other. But the uroboros was hardly confined to

China and Egypt, and in fact appeared in a wide variety of cultures—African, Norse, Aztec, Native American, and Hindu, among others (figure 3.2).

Figure 3.1. "One is all," from Codex Marcianus.

Figure 3.2. Aztec uroboros.

From Egypt, the symbol passed into Greek culture, much as other alchemical and prealchemical ideas did, as we've seen. The word *uroboros* (one of several spellings) comes from the Greek for "tail-eater." In the *Timaeus*, Plato described the first living being in terms strikingly similar to the uroboros. He said that this first being had neither eyes nor ears because it was totally self-contained, with nothing external yet in existence. Its waste was also its food, which in turn became waste, in a closed ecological cycle. It was perfect in its self-sufficiency.

For Christian Gnostics, the uroboros represented the limits of the material world and a life based on material goals. An early Gnostic document, *Pistis Sophia*, puts it this way: "The outer darkness is a great dragon, whose tail is in his mouth, outside the whole world and surrounding the whole world,"[3] and this: "The disk of the sun was a great dragon whose tail was in his mouth and who reached to seven powers of the Left and whom four powers in the form of white horses drew."[4]

It was intrinsic to alchemy that the final product of the opus—the philosopher's stone—was already contained in its beginning—the *prima materia*. Thus the uroboros served as the perfect alchemical symbol to express the idea that "one is all." Because it fit so perfectly the alchemical ideal, we encounter the uroboros not only as a symbol of the total opus, but also in variations used to symbolize a wide variety of alchemical truths. For example, in an extensive series of eighteenth-century woodcuts by Johann Conrad Barchusen,[5] the tail-eater occurs at virtually every stage of the alchemical process. In the selection of images shown in figure 3.3, the snake begins as a tail-eater, then unwinds and burrows into the philosopher's egg* to fertilize it. Within the egg, it then bites its tail again, forming a new unity. In a number of pictures, corresponding to stages in the alchemical process, the snake is hidden within the egg. Eventually it emerges and bites its tail to form a circle around the egg. In some of these stages, the egg transforms into an alchemical vessel, the better to make an explicit point that this series of images is symbolizing an actual physical process performed by the alchemist.

This set of pictures of the uroboros (and I stress that there are many more pictures, both with and without the uroboric image, within the total series) goes out of its way to stress that the end of the process is already contained at the beginning. Nevertheless, without the process, the final product cannot be created. There has to be an incubation, a fertilization,

---

* The philosopher's egg is a frequent image in alchemy for the developing philosopher's stone, which is the final product of the opus. We'll see more on this in chapter 6.

Figure 3.3. Barchusen woodcut.

and then much work before the philosopher's egg becomes the completed philosopher's stone. The final pictures in Barchusen's cycle show the final product contained within the boundaries of the uroboros.

In alchemy, Hermes Trismegistus (i.e., "Thrice Greatest Hermes," whom we encountered in the previous chapter) is known as Mercurius. Mercurius presides over every step of the opus and serves as a symbol of the transformative power that connects opposites. Since everything in alchemy has both a symbolic and a literal meaning, Mercurius also represents the chemical element mercury, also commonly known as quicksilver, the only metal found in nature in liquid form. Mercury was known to early civilizations and was found in Egyptian tombs as early as 1500 BC. It combines with gold and silver (and with most other metals, except iron) to form a soft amalgam, that is, an alloy that contains mercury. A common ancient way to extract gold from crushed crude ore was to add mercury, so that the gold formed an amalgam with the mercury. Further processes were then used to extract the mercury from the amalgam, leaving the gold. Mercury thus seemed a perfect symbol for all alchemical transformation. As such, it fascinated those who discovered it, much as it still does the child who encounters it for the first time. The alchemists stress, however, that their mercury is not the normal mercury known to others.

In alchemical imagery, Mercurius is often combined with the uroboros in subtle ways. In some of the alchemical drawings, the snake that fertilizes the philosopher's egg is three headed to indicate that it is actually Mercurius who is the transformative agent (figure 3.4). For alchemists this image was a shorthand way to indicate that mercury was necessary to begin the process.

Figure 3.4. Mercurius as uroboros.

One of many variants on the uroboros in alchemy is the bird who eats itself. Images show a pelican pecking away at its own chest, often with drops of blood showing, to demonstrate the difficulty experienced in the alchemical work (figure 3.5). This particular image also represented a particular kind of alchemical vessel, called the pelican, in which a tube led back from the top of the vessel into the middle of the vessel. When heated, this shape created a circulation of the mixture within.

Figure 3.5. Pelican pecking its chest and a pelican vessel.

The twentieth century has given us perhaps the most perfect image of the circulatory process represented by the pelican: the mathematical object known as a Klein bottle (figure 3.6). The outside of a Klein bottle is also the inside. If you filled a Klein bottle with water, the water would flow along the outside of the bottle onto the floor. Or you could just as easily dip the outside into a pail of water to fill up the inside. Unfortunately, a Klein bottle cannot exist in our three-dimensional world; we would need a fourth spatial dimension to create it. This is, however, the impossible situation that the alchemists were trying to capture in their uroboric images.

Still another variant on the figure of the uroboros was to have the snake form a figure eight, with one circle above another, before biting its tail. In this way, the uroboric image also conveys "as above, so below." A mathematical equivalent of this image is a Möbius strip (named after its discoverer, nineteenth-century German mathematician August Möbius). To make a Möbius strip, take a long, narrow strip of paper. Bring the two ends together and glue them to make a circle; however, just before you glue

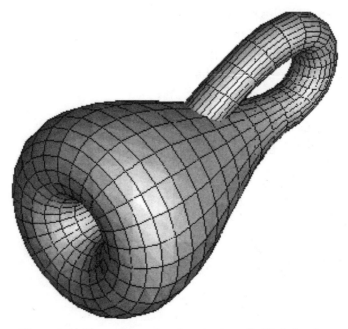

Figure 3.6. Three-dimensional projection of a Klein bottle.

them together, give one end a single twist. That single twist transforms a two-dimensional figure—a circle—into a one-dimensional figure—a Möbius strip! Let's say you want to color the outside of the strip red and the inside blue. Take a red felt-tip pen and start coloring the outside. Keep sliding the strip along as you color it. Unless you've seen a Möbius strip before, you should be very surprised when you eventually arrive back at your starting point. "Both" surfaces of the strip are colored red, because there is really only one surface. There's no inside left to color blue. Magicians perform a trick called the Afghan Bands that is based on the principle of the Möbius strip. Instead of paper bands, they use strips of cloth, which are easy to tear along their length. One strip is joined into a simple circle. A second is given the twist that transforms it into a Möbius strip before its ends are joined. Both look like simple circles of cloth. When the true circle is torn in half lengthwise, two circles of cloth result. However, when the Möbius strip is torn, you end up with one circle that has a diameter twice the size of the original circle. An anonymous limerick says it this way:

A mathematician confided
That a Möbius strip is one-sided.
You'll get quite a laugh
If you cut it in half,
For it stays in one piece when divided.

In one further variant of the alchemical uroboros, the figure eight was formed by a single tail biter above and two tail biters biting each other's tails below (figure 3.7). Not only does this show the idea of "as above, so below," but we might speculate that there are three tail biters to show Mercurius in some intermediate process in which, while joined, he is also split in some complex way.

Figure 3.7. Uroboros combining two and three.

As we will discuss at length in the final chapter of this book, the later alchemists were quite aware that the opus was as much a transformation of the alchemist as it was a physical transformation in the laboratory.

"In the age-old image of the uroboros lies the thought of devouring oneself and turning oneself into a circulatory process, for it was clear to the more astute alchemists that the *prima materia* of the art was man himself."[6]

Mandalas

The universal containment process of feedback has been symbolized from ancient times by a *mandala*. Mandalas appear as sacred symbols of more-than-human wholeness that occur ubiquitously across cultures, old and new. Though not as central a symbol as the uroboros in alchemy, they still occurred widely in symbolic alchemical pictures. *Mandala* is a Sanskrit word meaning "circle," and, in fact, most mandalas are circular, though some have squares or other geometric shapes as the outer container (figure 3.8).

Figure 3.8. Tantric yoga mandala.

In the most common of all mandala patterns, square patterns are contained within circular patterns.

A circle or sphere seems to be an almost universal symbol for the perfection of the godhead (recall Pascal's phrase that "God is an infinite sphere" from the previous chapter). And four—as in the sides of a square—is a symbol for wholeness. For example, as a famous alchemical axiom, attributed to third-century alchemist Maria Prophetissa, has it: "one becomes two, two becomes three, and out of three becomes the one as the fourth." But this idea predates alchemy. In the central text of Taoism, the *Tao Te Ching*, which dates to the fourth century BC,[7] Lao Tzu taught:

> The Way begot one,
> and the one, two;
> Then the two begot three
> And three, all else.[8]

Jungians frequently refer to this concept because it shows the stages of development in dealing with almost any issue within the psyche. "The one" is the stage in which something is unconscious, undifferentiated. Next a polarity always arises as the issue moves into consciousness. If tension is held between the opposites long enough, the third appears as the movement out of the tension. Finally, when the issue is fully integrated into the personality as the fourth, the transformed personality is a new whole and, as such, is the starting point for any further change. Jung noticed that when his patients reached a critical point where a new level of wholeness was trying to emerge, mandalas began to show up in their dreams; he would encourage them to draw those patterns, as he himself did at a similar stage of his own development (and as I myself did).

Jung speculated that, as a combination of circle and square, mandalas reflect an attempt by the psyche to bring the limited wholeness possible to the individual (the square) into synchrony with the Self (the circle). In mathematics, this same inner need for wholeness took the form of the search to "square the circle," that is, to construct a square with the same area as a circle, using only the algebraic equivalents of compass and straight edge. This seemingly simple (though impossible) problem occupied mathematicians for more than five thousand years! Perhaps the root of their fascination was this: even though a square can never achieve the perfection of a circle, it can approach perfection as closely as desired. For example, imagine that a square progresses to an eight-sided polygon, then a sixteen-sided polygon, and on and on, until the polygons has so many sides that, to the naked eye, it appears like a circle. But it is important to realize that no matter how long the process continues, the progression of polygons will never actually become a circle; that perfection remains an unattainable goal.

Mandalas are frequent objects of meditation in traditions Eastern and Western. The eye is drawn around the mandala, ever repeating the inner need to unite the square with the circle. The fact that the two never fully unite creates an inner tension within the psyche of the meditator. We now have a complementary pair of symbols. The uroboros presented an alchemical image of the feedback process in which both the goal and the process to reach the goal were contained within the starting point. In contrast, the mandala presented an alchemical image of a feedback process that could reach ever closer to a final goal, without ever fully reaching it.

CHAOS THEORY: CYBERNETICS

Should one name one central concept, a first principle, of cybernetics, it would be circularity.

—Heinz von Foerster[9]

We have already seen the centrality of feedback in chaos theory a number of times. In chapter 1, we encountered nineteenth-century mathematician Henri Poincaré, who discovered, to his dismay, that because of feedback the movements of even three heavenly bodies could not be predicted fully. In the 1960s, meteorologist Edward Lorenz realized that "any physical system that behaved nonperiodically would be unpredictable,"[10] again because of feedback. We will see another example in the next chapter, when we consider systems that can be depicted in a "bifurcation diagram." In these systems, feedback leads to bifurcations,* then to chaos, then finally to the emergence of a new, self-referential order.

With fractals and the ultimate fractal, the Mandelbrot set, feedback led not to chaos† but to creative preservation of self-referential structure, which we will encounter in more depth when we deal with the concept of autopoiesis in chapter 6. But before chaos theory and autopoiesis, there was cybernetics (from the Greek for "pilot" or "steersman"), which is the explicit study of feedback. There would be no chaos theory without cybernetics, and cybernetics provides key insights into what makes feedback so significant a part of reality:

> When [Norbert] Wiener brought the feedback idea to the foreground, not only did it become immediately recognized as a fundamental concept, but it also raised major philosophical questions as to the validity of the cause-effect doctrine . . . and a possibility of understanding teleology . . . Since Wiener, the analysis of various types of systems has borne this same generalization: Whenever a whole is identified, its interactions turn out to be circularly interconnected, and cannot be taken as linear cause-effect relationships if one is not to lose the system's characteristics.[11]

The scientific field of cybernetics first emerged from the fertile mind of mathematician Norbert Wiener soon after the end of World War II.‡ But though the important early concepts of cybernetics were already formulated by Wiener (and his key collaborator Arturo Rosenblueth), it was really the Macy Conferences—a series of ten interdisciplinary conferences beginning in 1946 and continuing through 1953—that took cybernetics from the idea stage to a fully developed field, largely through the tension of two different points of view represented at these conferences.

---

* A bifurcation is merely a division into two branches, as when a road suddenly branches off in two directions.

† At least not in general: chaos does emerge at the edges of the Mandelbrot set, a fact that we did not explore.

‡ Norbert Wiener and John Stuart Mill, who we'll mention in chapter 5, are probably the two best-known child prodigies who went on to successful adult lives. Wiener recorded his story in his book *Ex-Prodigy* (New York: Simon and Schuster, 1953).

Historian Steve J. Heims calls the two sides the "cyberneticians" and the "social scientists."[12] During World War II, social science had moved out of the college classroom and beyond theory into application, because the ideas of psychologists, anthropologists, and sociologists were needed in the war effort. The Macy Conferences marked the first time that "hard" scientists and "soft" scientists came together to discuss a single idea, each trying to offer his or her own unique perspective.

What was so important about cybernetics that it could unite such a varied group? It was something entirely new in human thought, "a general concept, or more precisely, a model, that encompassed certain engineering devices as well as aspects of human behavior."[13] It was the first time that the behavior of humans and other living creatures was consciously compared with how machines function, not to reduce human beings to machines, but to see whether the analogy could yield new insights into behavior. This approach broke totally from the previous behaviorist emphasis on stimulus-response chains, which in effect looked at all behavior as a series of causally connected events. In contrast, this new model "was concerned with goal-directed actions, where an organism acts with a purpose . . . Second, the model replaced the traditional cause-and-effect relation of a stimulus leading to a response by a 'circular causality' requiring negative feedback."[14]

Previously science had relegated ideas of goal directedness—teleology—to the scrap heap of such prescientific notions as vitalism or spontaneous generation. Scientists felt that cause and effect, building ineluctably from past causes to future effects, could explain all. Cybernetics supplied a new way of viewing reality that lent itself to scientific description and even mechanical realization, yet could deal with situations too complex for simple causality to explain. To understand the idea at its simplest level, imagine a thermostat regulating air-conditioning. The thermostat will continuously compare the actual temperature—let's say it's 75 degrees—with the desired temperature at which you have set the thermostat—70 degrees in our example. As long as the actual temperature is above the desired temperature, the air-conditioning will come on and stay on. When the actual temperature reaches 70 degrees, the thermostat will shut off the air conditioning. It will stay off until the temperature once more climbs above the desired setting (usually by a preset amount, such as 2 degrees). All this will be done in a mechanical manner that doesn't involve itself with philosophical issues like teleology. Even our little thermostat already involves both the key concepts in cybernetics: positive and negative feedback. Positive: keep doing what you're doing; negative: stop what you're doing. Seen in that light, cybernetics hardly seems startling, but it was a major break from Newtonian dynamics.

As an aside, I once read that Richard Nixon liked to sit in his den with the air-conditioning set to 60 degrees and a fire in the fireplace. I like to imagine that the fireplace was also artificial and increased its heat level any time the temperature in the room was below, say, 60 degrees. The two cybernetic systems could then fight to the death until, perhaps, a bifurcation would take place and it would snow in his den!

To get a clearer perspective on the nature of feedback, let's meet two very different attendees of the Macy Conferences, one each from the "cyberneticians" and the "social scientists." Representing the cyberneticians is psychiatrist and research physiologist Warren McCulloch, who collaborated with boy genius (well, almost a boy, as he was only twenty at the time) Walter Pitts to create the McCulloch-Pitts model for neural networks in the human brain.[15] Theirs was the first "computer" model of the brain. What is truly remarkable is that the concept predated actual computers; all references in McCulloch and Pitts' original paper were simply to mathematical logic. They viewed the neurons in the brain as binary devices that could receive either excitatory or inhibitory inputs from the synapses. When the value of these inputs passed a certain threshold, a neuron would turn either on or off. If enough of these simplified neurons are linked together into a closed network, McCulloch and Pitts proved, a large class of logical problems can be solved. Essentially, they presented the brain as a universal Turing machine,* or what we now call a computer. In effect, they viewed the brain as an incredibly complex feedback loop,

---

* Named for British mathematician and cryptographer Alan Turing, who in 1954 tragically committed suicide at the height of his powers. During the worst of the Cold War paranoia, he had been convicted of being a homosexual by the British government.

composed of numerous smaller feedback loops that branched from it. Now, in reality, neurons are a good deal more complicated than the McCulloch-Pitts model, but their paper sparked the whole field of research into "connectionist" or feedback models of the brain, which continues to this day. It also had a great deal to do with the creation of actual computers.

In his youth, after studying Bertrand Russell's massive *Principia Mathematica*, in which mathematics was viewed as a subset of logic,[*] McCulloch was tantalized by this deep philosophical question: "What is a man that he can know a number?" Attempting to answer that question led him into first psychology, then neurophysiology, but it was the power of logic that primarily drove him. In his cybernetics work, he joined with Pitts, who was an autodidact who could master a new field not in years or even months, but often in days. Even gifted scientists would defer to Pitts for a logical analysis of an issue within their own fields. McCulloch served as a father figure for Pitts (as did Norbert Wiener, though to a lesser extent).[†] Together McCulloch and Pitts made an impressive single representative for the power of logic. But as we'll see in chapter 5, logic isn't everything.

Anthropologist Gregory Bateson was an equally impressive spokesman for the other camp. He grew up in an almost overwhelmingly intellectual British family. At one time or another, virtually all the major intellectual figures in Britain and Europe sat at the Bateson dinner table, engaged in deep discussions on the important subjects of the time. His father was a famous, albeit controversial, British biologist who is best remembered for championing the rediscovery of nineteenth-century monk Gregor Mendel's pioneering work in genetics. Growing up with biological issues in his bones, Bateson initially chose zoology as a field, then moved on to anthropology, to which he brought an ecological point of view long before ecology existed as a field. Heims characterizes Bateson as a "scout": someone exploring new territory in advance of the group. He did this not only

---

[*] Mathematician Kurt Gödel later proved this view to be wrong, as we will see in chapter 5.

[†] Pitts, in contrast with Wiener, did not go on to a distinguished adult career. Instead he gradually fell into a schizophrenic state and withdrew from all relationships and work.

Walter

P... actor Michael Pitts (Murder by N°, & Berlgusconi's

for the Macy group, but also throughout his career. "From anthropology and learning theory he moved to psychiatry, behavior of otters and octopus [sic], theory of humor, kinesics, language and learning among dolphins, and theory of evolution."[16]

Bateson felt that the basic premise Wiener and his colleagues presented could open up a brand new approach to all the "soft sciences." It offered a way to talk about complex interactions among people, their environment, and the information that was being exchanged and to do so precisely, within a mathematical symbolism. Throughout the remainder of his life, Bateson drew on a cybernetic approach, emphasizing the fact that all living creatures, and all groupings of living creatures, can be viewed as complex feedback systems. Any such system provides information to itself about its performance, which in turn is used to change that performance. That change leads to further feedback, thus forming a continuous loop. So far, this differs little from our earlier example of a thermostat. The information the system feeds back to itself so it can better adapt to reality is, however, of a higher order of reality than the behavior that it comments upon. Hence living creatures are complex self-referential systems.[17]

Bateson and McCulloch often came at issues from totally different perspectives. Surprisingly, though, they agreed on the centrality of "empathy." Both seemed inherently to understand that empathy is a necessary feedback mechanism for interaction with other living beings. Bateson drew on it extensively in his later work with dolphins. McCulloch went so far as to argue that empathy should extend even to inanimate objects like our tools. In these days of personal computers and cell phones, this idea surely seems less strange than it did when he proposed it.

At the Macy Conferences, Bateson drew on his background as an anthropologist and often presented examples of cybernetic feedback mechanisms in various cultures, "including the case of the Iatmul culture in which a transvestite ceremony served as a homeostatic mechanism whenever a characteristic pattern of aggressive actions within the tribe threatened to divide them."[18] That might seem like pretty small stuff in comparison with the McCulloch-Pitts model, which led to the contemporary scientific area of neural nets. But Bateson's ability to cut across academic disciplines allowed him to scout out new areas of thought, to sniff out what was important, to ask the central questions before anyone else even knew there was anything to be asked. Of course, like all scouts, once a new field—like cybernetics—achieved respectability, his questions were, unfortunately, often dismissed as irrelevant by those more intent on the matters at hand. We are only now coming to reexamine questions Bateson raised half a century ago. For example, in his own work, he distinguished "learning" from "learning to learn" ("proto-learning" and "deutero-learning," respectively). Applying that idea to computers, Bateson asked the group "whether computers can learn to learn, and how in a formal mathematical way one could distinguish that from plain learning."[19]

Through the decade of the Macy conferences, and beyond them until his death in 1980, Bateson continued to extend the scope of these cybernetic questions. In 1968, fifteen years after the last Macy conference, he organized a conference on the Effects of Conscious Purpose on Human Adaptation. As an introduction, he offered eleven "considerations." The first seven discuss cybernetic systems in general. The last four move into the relationship between mind and world and are thus of more concern for us:

8. The content of the screen of consciousness is systematically selected from the enormously great plethora of mental events. But of the rules and preferences of this selection, very little is known . . .

9. It appears, however, that the system of selection of information for the screen of consciousness is importantly related to "purpose," "attention," and similar phenomena which are also in need of definition, elucidation, etc.

10. If consciousness has feedback upon the remainder of mind and if consciousness deals only with a skewed sample of the events of the total mind, then there must exist a systemic (i.e., non-random) difference between the conscious views of self and the world and the true nature of self and the world. Such a difference must distort the processes of adaption.

11. It is suggested that the specific nature of this distortion is such that the *cybernetic nature of self and the world tends to be imperceptible to consciousness. . . .*[20]

In other words, we don't know where our conscious ideas come from and what the selection process is for them. What we want to do and where our attention is both have an effect on that selection, but we don't even know what causes us to direct our attention to something, to desire one thing and not another. All we have to deal with consciously are the results of those selections, over which consciousness has no choice. Yet we proceed as if we are able to consciously understand both what goes on in the world outside us and what we are like inside. We are unaware that both inner and outer worlds might be quite different from what we think them to be.*

Even so, both hard science and social science could ask good questions and push toward important results. In that same 1968 conference, a now-aged Warren McCulloch suggested that what was needed for a resolution of these cybernetically self-referent problems was "a logic of relations," and he felt that "such a logic looks to be pretty well underway."

> The great problem is the context. We've all tried to handle context as though it were a general background, but when you look at a calculator, it appears in the form of an operator . . . [I]f we can handle the context properly as an operator in our logic, I think we're going to go some places.[21]

When someone asked him for an example of a context as an operator, McCulloch gave this wonderful example.

> A man meets a girl and he asks her to take off her clothes. If it's a cocktail party, it's a dare; if it's a boudoir, it's the right thing; if it's in a streetcar, he's a pervert. The moment you take the context in, it decides how you deal with the rest of it. It behaves as an operator in a strictly formal sense. It doesn't come in as a vague background.[22]

---

* See more about this difference in the next section in the discussion of the dynamics of the psyche in Jungian psychology.

Chapter Three

LESSONS FOR SELF-TRANSFORMATION

Psychologically, circulatio is the repeated circuit of all aspects of one's being, which gradually generates awareness of a transpersonal center uniting the conflicting factors. There is a transit through the opposites, which are experienced alternately again and again, leading finally to their reconciliation.

—C. G. Jung[23]

The image of feedback in both alchemy and chaos theory illustrates two central truths for all self-transformation: (1) the end is already present at the beginning, and (2) there is no way to short-circuit that process; we have to work through the same issues over and over, always coming back to the same point. But—and this is the essence of the process—when we come back to the starting point each time, the starting point has changed. The process of self-transformation isn't a straight path toward a goal; it's a spiral in which we circle ever closer to our final goal.

We can see this pattern illustrated most clearly in Jungian psychology, which has been used extensively to study the dynamics of this process. Jungian psychology stresses the difference between the ego, which is the center of consciousness, and the Self, which is the center of the total psyche, both conscious and unconscious. The process of individuation is described as the *circumambulatio of the Self.* One image of this process (though, of course, there is no way to fully capture it) is to imagine the Self as an upright pole in the center, with the ego moving in a clockwise spiral around the Self. Each time it returns to the same place in the circle around the Self, but it has moved higher and closer. As it continues, the ego comes closer and closer to the Self, without ever reaching it. This relatively simple image is an attempt to show that the process is not simply a linear progress toward a goal.

Many further particulars in both alchemy and chaos theory speak to how feedback operates in the process of transformation. In alchemy, as we mentioned in passing earlier in this chapter, paired operations are cycled through over and over during the course of the opus. In the next chapter, we will deal with two primary operations that take something apart, then put it back together: the *solutio* (dissolving), followed by the *coagulatio* (coagulating, thickening). But three operations are themselves explicit illustrations of feedback: the up-and-down movements of the *sublimatio* (sublimating, aerating, rising, making more spiritual), the *mortificatio* (mortifying, falling into matter) that follows *sublimatio*, and especially the *circulatio* (circulating, continual cycles of rising and falling).

As we discussed in the previous chapter, all too often spiritual traditions glorify the spirit at the expense of the body and try to show the spiritual path as one in which the body and its needs are discarded as we climb higher and higher. In the alchemical model, as we grow in spirituality (the *sublimatio*), we need to follow that with a grounding in the body (the *mortificatio*). A *circulatio* needs to take place in which we continually alternate an upward movement with a downward movement.

I once gave a lecture on Neoplatonism in which I tried to illustrate the problem of assuming that we can simply keep moving higher and higher, discarding our seemingly nasty lower selves as we go. I held up a length of rope and suggested that the top represented our spiritual side and the bottom our instinctual side. "Let's cut off that inferior lower end." After cutting, I pointed out that the rope that remained still had both an upper end and a lower end. I continued cutting off the bottom end, but no matter how many times I cut it, the rope still had two ends. At the conclusion, there was only a tiny little piece of rope left in my hand. I concluded by saying, "That's the circumstance in which we find ourselves if we condemn our instinctual nature and simply try to cut it off from our lives. It doesn't go away; it can't. Instead we find ourselves becoming smaller and smaller people, until there's not enough left of us to accomplish anything worthwhile in our lives. And that's sad."

We should also note how varied the appearance of the uroboros becomes during the alchemical opus. It forms the initial container, then it burrows into the alchemical egg that begins the process. It vanishes for a while, then it reemerges, finally wrapping itself around the completed philosopher's stone. We find all those instances (and many other variants) during the process of self-transformation. Just as the uroboros forms the initial container, we are often graced at the beginning of our journey with a view of the whole process. For example, therapists often notice that the initial dream brought by a patient lays out the whole course of therapy. In the words of Jungian analyst Kate Marcus, "In some of the creation myths which tribes or peoples have 'dreamed' about their world coming into being out of a state of pre-existence, one may detect an archaic prefiguration of the people's collective destiny. In a similar way it seems possible to detect in some initial dreams a prefiguration of a person's individual destiny."24

After the initial glimpse of the whole process, like the uroboric snake, the process can burrow within us, leaving us feeling without any direction, lost in a meaningless process. Only later, without our conscious intervention, does it reemerge in wholeness. This dynamic illustrates that we have to keep working away at the process, going over and over many of the same things, while the transformative process is proceeding in our unconscious. They say talk is cheap; well, so is conscious insight. Most often the transformative process takes place not because we come to a conscious insight about the process—the insights come long afterwards, if at all—but because we simply do our work, trusting that there is a purpose to the process and that something bigger than us will transform us.

In the previous chapter we mentioned that if the snake is given a twist before biting its tail, the image prefigures the mathematical figure of a Möbius strip. Though the Möbius strip appears to be a two-sided figure, with both an inside and an outside, we saw that if we try to color the outside red and the inside blue, the whole figure ends up red. The inside is the outside. That truth is a central understanding of self-transformation: our inside and outside are one, and it is only our mistaken consciousness that thinks otherwise.

Chaos theory and cybernetics support these alchemical insights, but they also offer unique points of their own about the centrality of feedback in transformation. The alchemical idea that the end of the opus is already contained with its beginning had been long discarded by science under the pejorative term *teleology*, that is, the idea that natural events occur by design, for a purpose. Darwin's brilliant discovery of evolution by natural selection seemed to science to have put an end to this idea. From then on, the world was pictured as simply chaotic, with chance differences leading to final change through the action of natural selection. We should, at least theoretically, be able to follow the chain of causal events, beginning with some random change, to its final conclusion. We've already seen that chaos theory exposed one fault in this view: tiny random changes at the beginning can lead to final events that cannot be presented in a logical chain, even after the fact, and certainly not predicted in advance.

Cybernetics had, however, already pointed out the more central flaw: natural systems (like the weather, or fluid dynamics, or human behavior, or almost anything else complex enough to be of interest) do not form causal chains; instead nature forms feedback loops in which information is constantly fed back into the system. Nature is neither pushed by the past, nor pulled by the future; rather, it is impossible to separate the joint systems that form both the past and the future of any natural event. We each exist in an eternal moment that in some way contains both everything that came before and everything that will come, linked together in a complex feedback loop.

~Feedback~

4

Take Apart, Put Together

The sole sensation and understanding in the cosmos is to make all things and unmake them into itself again, an instrument of god's will.

—Corpus Hermeticum IX:6

C entral to both alchemy and chaos theory is the knowledge that for something to be transformed, it must necessarily be taken apart, then put back together in a new way. The classic image of such a transformation is the metamorphosis of a caterpillar into a butterfly, within the containment of a cocoon. It is important to remember that what emerges after the transformation must in some way already be contained within the original; as we'll find, however, it's not as simple as simply rearranging the parts. The process of taking apart and putting back together itself contributes to the transformation.

ALCHEMY

The alchemical regression to the fluid state of matter corresponds, in the cosmologies, to the primordial chaotic state, and in the initiation rituals, to the "death" of the initiate.

—Mircea Eliade[1]

Solutio and *Coagulatio*

In the previous chapter, we saw how operations in alchemy repeat, each time feeding back the results of previous operations. Two pairs of alchemical operations first take apart, then put back together: *solutio* (i.e., dissolve) and *coagulatio* (coagulate, come together), or *separatio* (break into parts) and *coniunctio* (conjunction, joining). Often the latter two—*separatio* and *coniunctio*—are subsumed as subelements within *solutio* and *coagulatio* (as are also the related operations of *sublimatio* and *mortificatio*). In fact, the alchemical opus was frequently summarized in the phrase "dissolve and coagulate," which indicates that many of the other operations could, if necessary, be subsumed within a more general view of *solutio* and *coagulatio*.

Alchemists accepted the Aristotelian model that all reality was composed of four elements: earth, air, fire, and water. During the course of the opus, the *prima materia* passed repeatedly through all four states of being. The *solutio* was the "water operation," in which solid matter was dissolved until it became liquid; the *coagulatio* was the "earth operation," in which the liquid once more became solid. Earth and water were thus linked in a cycle.* The paired operations of dissolve and coagulate were so primary that many alchemists felt that the opus did not begin until the *prima materia* was dissolved. For example, one alchemical text says that "until all be made water, perform no operation."[2]

Alchemy is replete with images for each of its processes, since each describes at one and the same time both a physical operation and a psychic process taking place inside the alchemist. Often the transitions between stages of the opus are represented by the coming together in various ways of the masculine, represented by the King or Sol (the sun), and the feminine, represented by the Queen or Luna (the moon). In our discussion of Mercurius in the previous chapter, we mentioned how gold and mercury formed an amalgam, from which gold could then be extracted. To begin this process, mercury, often called "first matter," was needed. Since pure mercury is rare in nature, it was most often extracted from cinnabar, which is a compound of mercury and sulphur. When cinnabar was subjected to intense heat in an alchemical furnace, the two elements separated. Since mercury had the magical property of being both metal and liquid,

---

* The other two of the four elements were represented by the operations of *calcinatio* (fire), and *sublimatio* (air).

alchemists theorized that it was the combination of sulphur and mercury in various proportions that could be transmuted into the various metals, such as silver and gold. The extraction of gold went like this. Once the mercury was created, the crude gold-containing ore was crushed and then dissolved in the mercury. As the ore dissolved in this transformative liquid, the mercury could bond to the gold in the ore, forming an amalgam. A distillation process then used heat to separate the mercury from the gold into separate beakers. A twelfth-century alchemical text described this process as dissolving Sol and Luna in "friendly water," which served as a womb, like the womb from which they had originally emerged. They could then be reborn, but "more healthy, more noble, and more strong."[3]

Many other images of *solutio* appear in the alchemical literature, some of which are less "friendly." Some of these show the influence of Egyptian mythology on alchemy. In the book of Genesis in the Bible, we learn the story of how Cain kills his brother Abel out of envy. Egyptian mythology includes a similar tale, which describes how the Age of Osiris gives way to the Age of Horus (just as another tale tells how the age of Ra gave way to the age of Osiris). At the beginning of the story, we learn that Osiris is the well-loved universal lord of the earth. Much like Cain, Osiris's brother Set is envious and wants that role for himself. Set tricks Osiris into climbing into a coffin on the slim pretext of seeing if he would fit. Once Osiris is in the coffin, Set closes and locks it, then cuts the coffin into fourteen pieces and casts the pieces into the water. (If this were an alchemical text, we would interpret it as telling the alchemist that he must first break the *prima materia* into small pieces, then dissolve them in water).*

With Osiris gone, Set makes himself ruler . . . but not for long, for his role is transitional in this story. Osiris' wife Isis hunts down all the pieces of her husband and brings them back together again. (In alchemical terms, this represents a *coniunctio*, a joining.) Once Osiris is reassembled, he is then reanimated just long enough to impregnate Isis with the seed of

---

* There are many variations on this myth. In some, instead of putting Osiris into a coffin and cutting it into pieces, he instead seals him in a lead coffin, which again would seem appropriate as an alchemical image.

Horus. The boy-god Horus is later born from this union. Eventually he fights with Set, wins, and takes over the rule himself.

Similar images of dismemberment appear in a variety of alchemical texts to symbolize the process of *solutio*. In some, in contrast to the Egyptian mythology, the wife, rather than being the healer, is herself the person who dismembers her husband. In still others, the wife joins with the husband and both are dismembered.

But more commonly the dissolving happens in the friendly territory of a bath or a pool. A good example can be seen in a famous series of ten alchemical drawings representing the complete process of the opus, called the *Rosarium Philosophorum*, which was published in Frankfurt in 1550. Three of the ten images are shown here (figures 4.1–4.3). Jung analyzed the drawings as psychological documents in *The Psychology of the Transference*.[4] They illustrate a *coniunctio* of opposites, leading to a *solutio*, followed by a *sublimatio* or *separatio*, and finally a *coagulatio* to form a final pure *coniunctio*. In an early stage of the process (figure 4.1), a *coniunctio* (a joining) is occurring between Sol and Luna within the bath.

Figure 4.1. *Rosarium*, stage 4.

A later stage (figure 4.2) shows the two dissolving into one being within the bath. In still a further advance, a *separatio* and *sublimatio* occurs in which

70

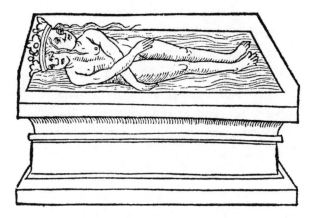

Figure 4.2. *Rosarium*, stage 6.

new life, represented by a child, rises from the bath to the heavens. Later it comes back to the bath to reinvigorate the moribund king and queen.

Finally, a newly transformed—and joined—Sol and Luna emerge (figure 4.3), surrounded by a variety of symbols to represent this transformation.

Figure 4.3. *Rosarium*, stage 10.

Among them you can see the three-headed snake we have already seen associated with Hermes Trismegistus.

The use of the image of the masculine and feminine dissolving to eventually form a hermaphroditic figure was intended to show that all opposites had to be joined together within the alchemical opus. In Jung's words, on the same problem in individuation, "The great problem in psychology is the integration of opposites. One finds this everywhere and at every level."[5]

Within alchemy, no matter how the images of *solutio* appear, they are always necessarily followed by some image of *coagulatio*. These two primary operations are also frequently combined with the operations of *separatio, sublimatio, calcinatio, mortificatio,* and *coniunctio*. The *coagulatio* can be accomplished in various ways, depending on the alchemical situation. Sometimes a cooling is needed, which causes the solid to form from the liquid; sometimes a heating (*calcinatio*) is needed to separate off the liquid (*separatio*); sometimes the addition of an additional substance is needed to allow the coagulation to occur. Three such coagulating agents were magnesia, lead, and sulphur. Though not mercury itself, these agents are all symbols of Mercurius in his role of crossing boundaries, in this case the boundaries between liquid and solid. Magnesia was a general term for a variety of impure mixtures that represented transitional stages of the opus. Lead was regarded as able to coagulate because it was itself heavy and dense. Isaac Newton said this about alchemical sulphur:

Inferior and superior, fixed and volatile, sulphur and quicksilver have a similar nature and are one thing, like man and wife. For they differ from one another only by degree of digestion and maturity. Sulphur is mature quicksilver, and quicksilver is immature sulphur: and on account of this affinity they unite like male and female, and they act on each other, and through that action they are mutually transmuted into each other and procreate a more noble offspring to accomplish the miracles of this one thing.[6]

Though these agents were each necessary at earlier "impure" stages of coagulation, the final coagulation was always clean and pure. For example, a sixteenth-century work (which was an influence on the *Rosarium* pictures shown above) said of these twin processes of *solutio* and *coagulatio*: "Unless the bodies lose their corporeal nature, and become spiritual, we shall make no progress with our work. The solution of a body takes place through the operation of the spirit, and is attended with the coagulation of the spirit. Then the body mingles with the spirit, and the spirit with the body."[7]

Raymond Lull's *Ars magna*

One of the remarkable characters in the history of alchemy is the Majorcan writer and philosopher Raymond Lull (1232/33–1315). Like St. Paul and St. Francis, Lull was born of wealthy parents and led a sybaritic life until converted by visions. Apocryphal stories about him abound. One concerns the manner of his religious conversion. It is said that while Lull was living as a nobleman at the court of James I, King of Aragon, by chance he glimpsed the bosom of a married noblewoman when her neckerchief was blown aside by the wind. He fell madly in love. He wrote her love letters, which she ignored, until he finally accompanied them with poems addressed to the beauty of her breasts. To persuade Lull that a man of knowledge should love only God, she agreed to show him the breasts he admired so much. When she opened her blouse and revealed her breasts, he saw that they were covered with a large cancer. His shock at the sight supposedly converted him to a religious life. He then began having visions that convinced him of his divine destiny to convert the Moslems to Christianity, and then to die himself as a martyr.[8]

Lull is known as a master alchemist, largely because his approach to astrological influence was adopted widely for several centuries. As with Nicolas Flamel, whom we will discuss in chapter 6, many later alchemical books were written by unknown authors using his name. His ideas in some ways anticipated those of Paracelsus nearly three centuries later, which we discussed in the previous chapter. In his books, Lull rails against the traditional approach to astrology, but then makes use of it in a way that, like Paracelsus, is perhaps closer to the later scientific temperament. In Lull's case, he connected the "elemental qualities in the seven planets and the twelve signs . . . with terrestrial elements" that could then be used for healing. That sounds much like Paracelsus.[9]

But it is another area of Lull's work that most interests us in this chapter. He was a strange combination of mystic and scientist, perhaps in that sense a precursor of those of us who find ourselves occupying that same uneasy middle ground at this turn of the twenty-first century. Living in the period overlapping the thirteenth and fourteenth centuries, Lull still worked from the medieval perspective of scholasticism, yet in many ways he was far closer to the Renaissance attitude toward the world that would later evolve into science. Like his contemporary St. Thomas Aquinas (his elder by ten years), Lull believed that "the divine law required man to see God by the rational methods of philosophy."[10] Yet he was also far ahead of his time, almost twentieth-century in some ways, and managed to develop an abstract method of extending knowledge through a primitive precursor of the computer. He developed this method of taking apart and putting together as a way to serve his visionary destiny of converting Moslems and Jews to Christianity.

His book *Ars magna* (Great art) presented graphic symbols "representing the primitive concepts which [he] planned to combine in order to express all other ideas and solve all problems of science, religion and philosophy."[11] Therein he presented "a mechanical method of exhaustively stating the possible relations of a topic."[12] There were many varieties of this mechanical method, incorporating three geometrical figures: the triangle (representing the divine Trinity), the square (representing the four elements), and the circle (representing the heavens). One of the most famous was a circular example, much like a dartboard with an inner circle, a middle circle, and an outer circle. Each circle is divided into sections. But unlike a dartboard, one of the circles is fixed while the other two circles can rotate freely around the center. By rotating the two moveable circles, any section of the outer circle can be paired up with any section of the middle circle and any section of the inner one. On one circle, he would put symbols representing relevant subjects, (e.g., the different things that exist, like God, man, angels, vegetation, etc.), on another symbols for relevant predicates (e.g., qualities like powerful, desirable, first, final, etc.), and in the last circle ideographs for various relevant questions (Whether? What? Whence? Why? How large? Of what kind? When? Where? How?). You could rotate the circles so that angels, powerful, and Why? were lined up, and you would be asking why angels are powerful.[13]

Obviously, you could make up particular examples of this device for virtually any subject that interested you. Lull was most interested in using the *Ars magna* to construct examples that would, he felt, demonstrate the infallibility of Christian doctrine, and thus prove the superiority of Christianity over Islam. We might think of it as a sort of missionary computer—something that would probably be welcomed today by all varieties of religious proselytizers. Lull lectured on this method widely throughout Europe.[14]

In the example in figure 4.4, he has written, in Latin, the Dignities of God on each of the bands. On the outer band, he simply used the letters B through K to stand for the same string of dignities. Though he used nine sections, a tenth was understood by omission: the ineffable name of God that cannot be written. The different bands could correspond to different levels of reality, from the various spiritual realms (including angels), to man, to the material world. By rotating the circles, he could talk about how different Dignities of God could connect at different levels. His art became incredibly complex in these analyses. Historian Frances Yates describes his devices this way:

> The figures of his Art, on which its concepts are set out in the letter notation, are not static but revolving. One of the figures consists of concentric circles, marked with the letter notations standing for the concepts, and when these wheels revolve, combinations of the concepts are obtained. In another revolving figure, triangles within a circle pick up related concepts. These are simple devices, but revolutionary in their attempt to represent movement in the psyche.[15]

Unfortunately for Lull, the *Ars magna* proved less infallible at demonstrating the superiority of Christianity than he would have hoped. In trying to convert the Moslems, he was twice imprisoned and banished, then finally stoned so badly he died soon afterwards on board a ship sailing to his home city of Palma, Majorca, where he was buried. At least he achieved his goal of dying a martyr, if not of converting the Moslems.

Lull interests us because his method presents an almost scientific version of taking apart and putting together. By rotating his different bands, he could illustrate a large number of possibilities; for example, in the case of the 9 x 9 x 9 device shown in figure 4.4, there are 729 possibilities. But one can easily imagine the number of disks and symbols on each disk growing ever larger, to the point where the logical machine approximates nature itself, with its seemingly endless possibilities for taking apart and putting together. The static world of the Middle Ages, in which knowledge was trapped in the same categories, never to be extended, was now in motion. Note, however, that a method like Lull's is insufficient to produce something totally new, like the philosopher's stone. It is only the dynamic quality of his device that is new.

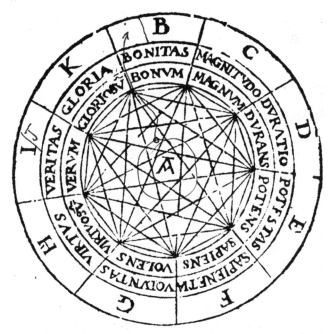

Figure 4.4. Raymond Lull's *Ars magna* computer.

Chaos Theory: Bifurcations and Attractors

*The evolution of complex systems can't be followed in causal detail
because such systems are holistic; everything affects everything else.
To understand them, it's necessary to see into their complexity.*
—John Briggs and F. David Peat[16]

Unlikely as it may sound, we're going to discuss chaos theory by discussing bread-making. Bread-making is a very ancient art, going back perhaps as much as 10,000 years, making it one of mankind's earliest important discoveries. Try to picture what happens when a baker kneads dough. The dough is pushed down until it's flat, then is folded onto itself, flattened again, then once more folded onto itself. This folding is repeated for just the right number of times, neither too few nor too many; knowing the right number for a given loaf of bread in different weather conditions is one of the many things that separates the artists among bread makers from the rest of the pack. This kneading process is necessary because when the gluten in the flour is rubbed together, it becomes elastic, which helps the bread rise.

As such, kneading bread is a perfect example of taking apart, then putting back together in a repetitive cycle. We will talk later in this chapter about "strange attractors," which are mathematical models of this behavior, but first let's talk about a process in chaos theory that explicitly takes the extremes, brings them together, takes the new extremes, brings them together, over and over. In this case, unlike the actual baker's work, the process continues infinitely. But to understand it, we need a short lesson in the difference between a traditional mathematical equation, which is timeless, and a dynamic equation, such as we find in chaos theory, which includes the effect of time.

Bifurcation Diagram or Logistics Map

In a traditional mathematical equation, if, for example, we want to know the area of a rectangle, we use an equation that says "area equals length times width" (i.e., $a = lw$). In mathematical terms, l and w are *variables*, meaning that you can vary the numbers you substitute for them and the equation still holds. If we want to know the distance we can travel at a certain velocity, the equation we use is "distance equals velocity times time" ($d = vt$). In using the computer to help model nature, a new type of *dynamic* equation is used in which the unknown on the left side of an equation is also one of the variables on the right side of the equation. This apparent impossibility is acceptable because it is implied that the variable on the right side is earlier in time than the variable on the left side.

This concept of introducing time as a resolution for problems of self-reference has become a commonplace through the wide use of computers. Computer programmers use the term "iteration" to describe the movement of a program from one state to another. For example, computer programs commonly count the number of times a subroutine has run by adding an instruction like $n = n + 1$, then checking the value of n to see if the subroutine has run enough times. It is understood that the n on the left side of the equation is a later stage than the n on the right side. Time has entered the picture. But note that this time is "dimensionless." We can't say that one n is a day or an hour or a minute or a second later than the other "n"; all we know is that one state of n is later than the other state.

I'll illustrate this with a classic example from chaos theory, one that begins with a very simple equation but yields surprisingly complex results, results that even lead to chaos. Unfortunately, there is no way to discuss chaos theory nontrivially without a teeny bit of math. So please bear with me for the next few pages, as there is actually some mathematics. But if you decide to skip past the math, you'll still be able to see and understand the results in graphic form.

Let's assume that we want to look at the growth of some animal population. We've all heard the phrase "breeds like rabbits," which implies that rabbits breed very fast. So we'll use rabbits and we'll oversimplify the situation.[17] We will use the letter R to stand for the number of rabbits at any point in time. And we'll use a mathematical convention that R has to be between 0 and 1. This convention makes the calculations easier; the results can always be multiplied later for the actual number of rabbits. Since this is an oversimplified situation, the only other number we'll need is the birthrate, and we'll let b be the variable that stands for the birthrate.

Let's make a first guess at how the rabbit population would grow over time by assuming that $R = bR$. That is, if we start with a rabbit population of R and a birthrate of b, after the breeding period, the new rabbit population will be bR. We put that new value of R into the equation on the right and calculate again. The process continues as long as we like. It's easy to see that, as long as the birthrate b is less than 1 (that is, more rabbits die than are born), the rabbit population would die out over time; if it is bigger than 1 (that is, more rabbits are born than die), the number of rabbits would grow and grow until the whole planet would be covered with rabbits. But in reality that doesn't happen; as the number of rabbits grows, they become more attractive to predators who eat them, allowing fewer to survive. And their food supply doesn't grow, so there is competition among the rabbits for the available food. The equation has to become more complex to deal with the fact that as the population grows, forces such as predators and competition for food act to make the population shrink.

We need something like the baker's transformation that makes things smaller when they get too big, bigger when they get too small. Let's add a new factor, $(1 - R)$, to the equation to account for the shrinking. Our new equation becomes $R = bR(1 - R)$. The expression $(1 - R)$ acts to shrink the population at the same time that R makes it grow.[18] Though this doesn't seem like a very big change, in fact, this simple addition makes for much more complex results. If we want to calculate the results for all starting values for the rabbit population R between 0 and 1, and all values of the birthrate b, the number of calculations is so huge that only a computer can deal with all the possibilities. Figure 4.5 shows the results; it is commonly called either a *logistics map* or a *bifurcation diagram*.

Let's look at some results on the logistics map. As we've already said, for birthrates below 1, the population dies out; for birthrates between 1 and 3.0, the number of rabbits will eventually reach a stable number and remain there. But, as you can see in the diagram, when the birthrate reaches 3.0, something remarkable begins to happen: the possibilities for the rabbit population begin to oscillate, first between two values, then between four

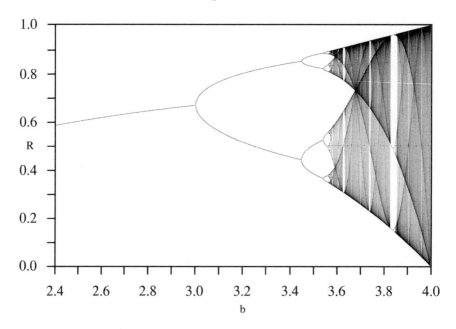

Figure 4.5. Logistics map or bifurcation diagram.

values, then eight, sixteen, and so on. This pattern is referred to as *period doubling*. If the resolution of the graph on the page were high enough and you had a sufficiently strong magnifying glass, you could watch the number of bifurcations rise higher and higher: 32, 64, 128, and on and on.

Another remarkable thing occurs at a point when the birthrate is approximately 3.57. The bifurcations stop and the results become totally chaotic; that is, there is no way of predicting where they will lie. When the birthrate reaches 4.0, the possibilities fill the entire surface between the extremes. And that isn't the end of the hidden mysteries revealed just by applying this simple equation over and over: if you look carefully, you'll notice white patches, smaller or larger, even after the point of chaos is reached. Again, if you had a really powerful magnifying glass, you would see that miniature versions of the entire diagram are hidden in those areas. You'd again see period doubling occurring, which eventually would lead to chaos.

In other words, as with the Mandelbrot set we examined in the previous chapter, "taking apart, putting together" in this mathematical way generates a self-referential figure, that is, a figure that again illustrates "as above, so below." If the "above" is the full graph, then the "below" is those smaller portions of the graph, the ones that look like the whole. Without intending to be sacrilegious, we could say that the god of the logistics map creates children in the god's own image.

Attractors

An *attractor* is a new concept that came out of dynamics in general and became central in chaos theory. It's a little hard to describe non-mathematically but easier to illustrate. One of the clearer definitions of an attractor is "a region on the domain of a dynamical system that attracts all nearby states." Since that is still a little abstruse, let's better define it through examples of the four main types of attractors.

The first is the *fixed-point attractor*. Imagine a bowl, then toss in a marble so that it circles the wall of the bowl. No matter where you throw it, no matter at what speed, eventually it will come to rest at a fixed point at the bottom of the bowl. Another example is a pendulum. If you start the pendulum swinging, it will move back and forth, but unless you have some way of continuing to add energy to the pendulum, the swings will become smaller and smaller over time, until the pendulum eventually comes to rest pointing straight down. That is again a fixed-point attractor. Since anything moving in a fixed-point attractor finally ends up resting at a single point, we can say that a fixed-point attractor is one-dimensional.

Take the same pendulum and assume that you can keep adding energy to it, as with the pendulum in a clock, so that each swing is exactly like the one before it, and the pendulum never comes to rest. If you give the pendulum a little push to one side, for a while its motion is out of line, but gradually it will return to the proper path and continue to trace the same path every time, with no variation. As another example, take a ball on a string and instead of swinging it back and forth like a pendulum, twirl it so that it traces a circular path. Again if no energy is added, it will eventually stop with the ball hanging down, evidence of a fixed-point attractor. But if the right amount of energy is added to the system, the ball keeps swinging in the same orbit, describing the same circle over and over. You can push it off-line a bit, but it will return to its proper orbit, like a planet in the solar system around the sun. These are both examples of *limit-cycle attractors*, since the only possible places where the system can go are "limited" and the behavior repeats, that is, it's "cyclic." A limit-cycle attractor is two-dimensional, since the path of any such attractor can be drawn on a plane.

Key to any attractor is that even if you can *perturb* the movement of the marble or the pendulum, give it a little push or pull away from its path, soon its movement will return to the attractor. As we found with the pendulum, if you push it so that it swings slightly askew, it will gradually return to its original movement. Without this feature, clocks would be highly unreliable.

The third type of attractor is called a *torus attractor*. A torus is a three-dimensional surface, shaped like the outside of a donut, with a hole in the middle, as shown in figure 4.6. Figure 4.7 shows a view of the torus from above, where it is easier to see that the torus is an extension of a limit-cycle attractor to a three-dimensional surface. The movement keeps wrapping around the surface and eventually coming back to its starting point after a varying number of spirals.

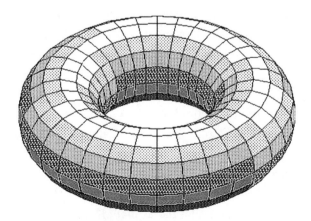

Figure 4.6. A torus.

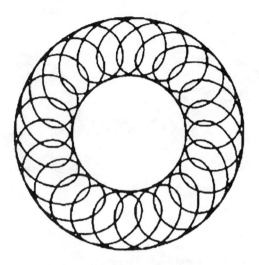

Figure 4.7. A torus seen from above.

Until chaos theory, these three attractors were considered to be the only types of attractors necessary to describe any dynamic motion. When systems became too complex to be described by a torus, for example, with fluid dynamics or wind dynamics or even the weather, the theory was that the torus would multiply into tori (the plural of *torus*) within tori, extending from three dimensions to four or five, endlessly. Thus, these three types of attractors would be sufficient to describe all of dynamics. As we will see, this model was wrong; a new and very strange attractor emerged, which came to be called, appropriately enough, a *strange attractor*.[19]

We have already encountered Edward Lorenz several times in previous chapters. His initial discovery of the butterfly effect was made using a model that had only twelve equations. He tried to see if he could create the same effect even more simply. Eventually he found he could reproduce it with only three equations that modeled fluid motion. (Recall that Henri Poincaré first discovered chaos when he attempted to solve the three-body problem.)

Figure 4.8 shows a view from one side of the three-dimensional attractor. It's wonderfully appropriate that the picture that illustrates the butterfly effect even looks like a butterfly. It's not obvious that it also illustrates

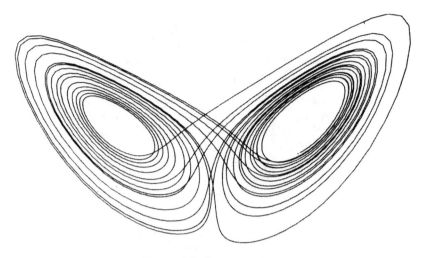

Figure 4.8. Lorenz attractor.

this chapter's examination of "take apart, put together," but it does so no less than the logistics map. Nearby trajectories come nearly together, then move away just as quickly. And they do so in unpredictable ways. No trajectory ever joins with its starting point to form a limit cycle. It's like an endless piece of thread that keeps wrapping around two invisible spools, moving back and forth between them, sometimes coming closer, sometimes moving farther away. (Of course, there is no actual equivalent of the two spools, just the dynamics of the system.) As with the baker's method of stretching and folding, nearby points are taken far apart, then distant points are brought close together.

You may remember from our discussion of fractals in chapter 2 that because coastlines are jagged, Mandelbrot realized that they had a dimension between 1 and 2. That is, they were more complex than a straight line, yet didn't totally occupy a two-dimensional plane. Similarly, a strange attractor can't be simply two-dimensional because when the folding brings trajectories together, if they touched, there might be a movement from one trajectory to the other. But the attractor isn't fully three-dimensional because it doesn't occupy the full three-dimensional space. Therefore, a strange attractor has a dimension between 2 and 3. As an oft-used example, consider the surface of a piece of paper, which is two-dimensional. Now crumple it up. It is now more complex than two dimensions, so it might have a fractal dimension of, perhaps, 2.5. If you crumple it until it's almost a solid ball, the fractal dimension will increase, approaching three dimensions but never quite reaching it. Earlier in this chapter we saw that the bifurcation diagram is fractal, which was probably not unexpected. But a second conclusion may be less obvious: *all strange attractors are also fractal!*

LESSONS FOR SELF-TRANSFORMATION

Few approach the process of self-transformation lightly. We come to it only when life has lost its zest and we feel heavy, leaden, depressed. Whichever way we move trying to escape our condition, we find a wall preventing further movement. There seems to be no "solution" to our problem. We try all the ways out that have worked for us in the past: denial of the situation, working so hard that we have no time to notice how we feel, throwing ourselves into hedonistic pleasures in the hope that they will make us feel better for at least a time.

None of them works. When we have exhausted all our conscious resources, we often find ourselves dissolving into tears, like we are experiencing a second adolescence. Those tears are a first step at dissolving our too-rigid personality structure into a "solution." It is within that "solution" that we begin the process of finding a "solution" to our condition. (The unconscious mind loves puns, and often seemingly innocent puns hold wisdom.)

Earlier I gave this alchemical quote: "Until all be made water, perform no operation."[20] This advice is no less true for self-transformation than for alchemical transformation. The "solution" into which we dissolve is the unconscious mind that lies within us.

Cut into Pieces

As we have seen, alchemy provides several metaphors for how that *solutio* takes place. One experience is like that of the Egyptian god Osiris, in that we can feel like we are cut into pieces and discarded. It's not merely that things fall apart in our lives; the process seems to cut us up, taking away each piece of our life separately. Many of us who have gone through a very deep transformative process can understand what that feels like. The resolution of this process of being cut into pieces isn't merely to reassemble the pieces of our personality, perhaps in some different order, with different priorities, like "I won't spend so much time on my career." Instead, the parts of our personality come together again to produce something new that may well take a long time to grow to fruition, much as the age of Osiris had to yield to the age of Horus. I've told the story of my own experience of being cut into pieces before, but it bears repeating because it's not an unusual story in our time.[21]

In my midthirties, I was happily married, a vice-president of computer software development and maintenance for a large firm, a man on his way up. I was smug and self-satisfied, convinced that my life would go from triumph to triumph. I saw myself as a Renaissance man, able to achieve success in the "bottom line" world of business, able to solve the complex intellectual problems presented by computers, yet also a person of taste and refinement, who appreciated books and music and art. I really thought I was something. Pride comes before the fall—the necessary transformative fall.

My philosophy—such as it was—could be summed up in a single phrase (as I had been fond of doing for a decade): "There ARE relative values!" That seemed very profound to me. By this phrase, I didn't imply only that all values are relative, that there are no absolutes. I also meant that relative values—human values—do have significance. They matter! Not a bad philosophy for a young man in his twenties—when I developed it. But hardly sufficient for the moral dilemmas that I was to encounter in my midthirties.

At the peak of my hubris, my best friend was fired, though not necessarily unfairly. A simple thing in the normal run of business; I had certainly fired enough people myself. Yet this was special because it was my best friend. I couldn't reconcile the event with my view of how I thought the world operated. Now when it was time for me to put my philosophy to the test ("there ARE relative values"), I found it painfully inadequate.

Without a moral base, I felt my whole understanding of reality tumbling around me. The one event was enough to cut me apart like a knife. It led me on a journey of nearly thirty years that is still underway, a journey in which, like Osiris, I was cut into many pieces and drifted on the sea of the unconscious. Every single thing I held stable in my life was taken from me one at a time. Amazingly, almost every single thing also came back when I was reassembled, but they had been transformed in previously unimaginable ways. In some ways, though, the person I became could have been recognized not only in the person I was before my long journey, but also in the young boy I once was. I have a picture of myself at four years old, and all the personality traits are already there.

Wheels within Wheels

Raymond Lull's mechanisms provide a different example of the transformative process. Though they appear relatively simple to our modern eyes, they provided the first *dynamic* method of examining different combinations of ideas. And they provide a different metaphor for the process of taking apart and putting back together. Imagine that inside us we have an enormously complex version of Lull's wheels within wheels. Each wheel would have symbols for all the unique aspects of our personality written around the edge: all the qualities we were born with and all those we have acquired through our life experience. Each wheel would, like Lull's example of the divine attributes, correspond to how those qualities relate to something different. Perhaps one would correspond to our relationships with our friends and family, another to our work life, another to our spiritual life, on and on. Imagine that the wheels are endlessly turning, presenting new combinations of how those same aspects could add up to a very different being. When a good combination comes up, which seems just right for our needs at some point in our life, the wheels stop turning and we settle into that combination. Then while we stay fixed with that combination in our conscious life, inside the wheels keep turning, examining not only our present needs, but projecting our future possibilities as well. Granted this model is oversimplified, but it does present a primitive version of the dynamics that actually seem to be going on within us all the time.

Attractors

The idea of attractors is one of the concepts from chaos theory that has attracted (so to speak!) writers from outside chaos theory itself. Everyone can relate to the idea that certain things serve as attractors in our life: sex, drugs, money, success. When we look at the drawing of the Lorenz attractor, it is easy to imagine that each of the two empty spaces is a different attractor that pulls us towards it. What is fascinating, though, about this attractor is that we can be orbiting closely around one side of the attractor, then suddenly around the other one. Often life presents us with such choices, and we are pulled toward one or the other possibility, engaging both by turns but never quite making up our mind fully. In the logistics map (figure 4.5), we can observe the result of being pulled one direction, then in the opposite direction. Whenever we go too far one way, we come back the other direction. The logistics map provides another way of seeing how this process can evidence itself in life. Often our life presents us with points of bifurcation; that is, we can go one way or the other, pulled by either of two attractors. Later two becomes four, four becomes eight. Then deterministic chaos occurs, and the possibilities are seemingly infinite. Sometimes, when the need for change is great enough, we simply descend into chaos, not knowing where we will come out. That trust is just as necessary for us as it was for the alchemists.

~Take Apart, Put Together~

5

Chaos and Emergence

Life is an emergent phenomenon, too—emerging from chemistry by way of DNA. . . . Emergent similarities "collapse chaos", they bring order to a system that appears to be wallowing hopelessly in a sea of random fluctuations.

—Jack Cohen and Ian Stewart

The starting point for this book was the moment when I read that, at a key point in the opus, alchemists would see flickering scintillae (i.e., sparks) of lights appearing in the darkness, like stars twinkling in and out of existence. This image struck me so strongly because it is almost exactly how chaos theory sees new form emerging from chaos. Neither in alchemy nor in chaos theory is it possible to know when and where the new will finally emerge, but both have this striking image of "new" beginning to appear in scattered fragments, some of which eventually coalesce into a whole. In this chapter, we're going to look at the stages from chaos to the emergence of new order, both in alchemy and in chaos theory.

ALCHEMY

In the language of the alchemists, matter suffers, until the nigredo disappears when the "dawn" (aurora) will be announced by the "peacock's tail" (cauda pavonis) and a new day will break, the leukosis or albedo. But in this state of "whiteness" one does not live in the true sense of the word, it is a sort of abstract, ideal state.

Chapter Five

In order to make it come alive, it must have "blood," it must have what the alchemists call the rubedo, the "redness" of life.

—C. G. Jung[1]

In earlier chapters we have seen that the alchemical opus involved the repetition of a variety of different operations, such as *solutio, coagulatio, sublimatio,* and so on. (Other lesser operations have not been described in this book.) What we haven't said so far is that these operations take place within a smaller number of progressive *stages*, and the operations have a different quality in different stages. All descriptions of the opus mention three such stages. First is the chaotic darkness of the *nigredo* (black). If the alchemist is successful in finding his way through the darkness, the *nigredo* eventually gives way to the *albedo* (white). The beginning of the *albedo* is often marked by an intermediate stage called the *cauda pavonis* (peacock's tail), which is characterized by a rainbow of colors. Then, if the alchemist continues to pursue his experiments successfully, both on the evolving *prima materia* and on himself, what finally emerges is the *rubedo* (red). Sometimes an intermediate stage occurs at the beginning of the *rubedo* called *citrinitas* (yellow; also called the *xanthosis*).* Thus there is a three-stage process from chaos to full life (and the philosopher's stone, which we will discuss in the next chapter).

Swiss philosopher Titus Burckhardt pointed out that this sequence is a natural one, from black as the "absence of colour and light"; to white, which is "undivided light"; and finally to red, which he calls "the epitome of colour."[2] Burckhardt added that "this ordering of things becomes even more evident, if between white and red . . . is inserted . . . a 'peacock's tail' of gradually unfolding colours." (Obviously Burckhardt places the *cauda pavonis* after the *albedo* rather than the *nigredo*.) Burckhardt also points out that in Hindu thought, "black is the symbolically 'downward' movement (*tamas*), which flees the luminous Origin; white is the 'upward' aspiration toward the Origin, toward the Light (*sattva*); and red is the tendency toward expansion on the plane of manifestation itself (*rajas*)."

---

* In some descriptions, the *cauda pavonis* follows the *albedo* and the *citrinitas* follows the *rubedo*. We won't deal with either substage in this book.

What is most important to realize is that each stage is qualitatively different from the one that precedes it, yet each emerges out of the previous stage. In other words, after a long period of operations that constitute one of the three stages, there is a marked transition to a very different stage. Chaos theory would call each shift to a new stage a *bifurcation*, since the new stage splits off from the old. Jung's final work on alchemy, *Mysterium Coniunctionis*,[3] concentrates on the conjunctions that occur to mark the end of one stage and the beginning of the next: (1) the mental union, which marks the culmination of the *nigredo*; (2) the union of mind and body, which marks the culmination of the *albedo*; and (3) the union of mind, body, and ultimate reality, which marks the culmination of the *rubedo* and the production of the philosopher's stone.

In psychological terms, the *nigredo* is the period of suffering and darkness (the "dark night of the soul" found in many spiritual traditions); the *albedo* is the period when one emerges from the dark night with new understanding. In the *albedo* stage, however, the adept's discoveries remain isolated from the normal world, like a hermit isolated on a mountaintop. During the *rubedo* stage, the hermit comes down from the mountaintop and slowly finds a way to integrate the new vision of life into the realities of the world we all live in.

The *Nigredo* (Chaos)

In the previous chapter, we explained that the entire opus was often reduced in alchemical literature to the phrase "dissolve and coagulate." The *prima materia*, the starting point, first had to be dissolved before the opus could really begin. Another way to view this step is to consider that dissolving the *prima materia* produces the stage of the *nigredo*, characterized by a chaotic lack of differentiation. In his important book *The Hermetic Tradition*, Julius Evola agrees, commenting that "the principle in question has a double meaning. It is Death and Life. It has the double power of *solve* and of *coagula*."[4] Johannes Fabricius quotes from Raymond Lull (whose *Ars magna* we discussed in the previous chapter), who described the *nigredo* as "black, blacker than black," with the additional comment: "and so it is an infinity."[5]

At this stage of nondifferentiation, nothing is also infinity; it is both empty and full because everything is contained within it *in potentia*. It has no qualities yet because only the act of distinction, of discrimination, can separate qualities out of this chaos. *This act of making a distinction is the birth of consciousness.*[6] Jung puts it well: "Nothing is the same as fullness. In the endless state fullness is the same as emptiness. The Nothing is both empty and full. One may just as well state some other thing about the Nothing, namely that it is white or that it is black or that it exists or that it exists not. That which is endless and eternal has no qualities, because it has all qualities."[7]

If the alchemist is inseparable from his experiments (as we will discuss in more detail in the following chapter), the true beginning point for the opus should be when the alchemist finds his hard-won certainties dissolving, leaving him in a period of inner turmoil, where nothing is certain any longer. This state of mind is depicted in figure 5.1 in a scene from *Atalanta fugiens*, a famous and unique 1618 alchemical volume by Michael Maier that includes pictures, epigrams, and musical fugues.[8] To quote Evola

Figure 5.1. *Nigredo* stage, from *Atalanta fugiens*, epigram 50.

again: "[Chaos is] the power of the undifferentiated, at whose touch all differentiation can be destroyed."[9] Commenting on the state of the alchemist during the *nigredo*, Johannes Fabricius quotes from the *Rosarium* that the "brain turns black."[10] It is difficult not to see this process in psychological terms, even if the alchemists only gradually came to that realization over many centuries. In an interview conducted by Mircea Eliade for a French magazine, *Combat*, Jung commented, "This work is difficult and strewn with obstacles; the alchemical opus is dangerous . . . 'Matter' suffers right up to the final disappearance of the blackness; in psychological terms, the soul finds itself in the throes of melancholy, locked in a struggle with the 'shadow.'"[11]

The modern word for this state is *depression*. During this stage, the alchemist's life energy was pushed down (i.e., literally depressed) into the unconscious. The alchemist had to live in that period of uncertainty for an unknown length of time before he emerged again into the light. Remember that his journey was a lonely one in which the alchemist was totally on his own, isolated from all those around him. The metalworkers, whom Eliade saw as the alchemist's predecessors, had their mystery guilds at least. Most other mystery traditions had secret societies in which masters could help guide initiates. But there were no alchemical guilds, no secret alchemical groups. There was only the alchemical literature, which was difficult to find and more difficult to understand. In trying to interpret that literature, the alchemist struggled with descriptions that were not only obscure, but also frequently contradictory (or at least they seemed so at this early stage of his understanding). When he attempted to put his reading into physical form in his experiments, he would often find that his experiments not only did not produce the expected results, but seemed to lead nowhere. As seventh-century hermit and alchemist Morienus said to King Khalid ibn Yazid:

> But one who has seen this operation performed is not as one who has sought it only through books, for there are books that mislead those in quest of this knowledge. And the greater part of those books are so obscure and disorganized that only those who wrote them can understand them. But he who is

eager for this knowledge and pursues it does well, for by means of it he will gain access to strange things he had never known before.[12]

And yet somehow, through this dark period, the alchemist had to hold on to an inner certainty that his task had meaning and could, with persistence, be accomplished. Only very gradually would the confusion begin to lessen and the alchemist pass through the *nigredo* toward the stage of whitening and clarity. Some scholars argued that the *nigredo* stage wasn't at the very beginning of the opus. It occurred instead only after the alchemist had reached a peak in his experiments and had experienced the pride that comes before a fall. He might start with high hopes, conduct some of the easier early experiments, then only gradually arrive at a state of confusion in which the initial clarity and certainty began to dissolve away. He would begin to feel as if he were adrift on a strange sea in a vessel with no rudder, no longer knowing where he came from, or where he was going. Whether the *nigredo* appeared at the start, or after some period of success, it was the critical stage that had to be undergone in order to progress further. It is only from within that chaos that the philosopher's stone could emerge.

In the introduction, we said that Jung considered the alchemical opus to be a psychological projection of the inner process of individuation that was taking place in the alchemist. The point corresponding to the *nigredo* in individuation is called the *shadow stage*. Shadow is a singularly appropriate word for a period when we are confronted with everything that we have previously denied within our personality, everything that previously was hidden in the shadows of our conscious existence. Just as the alchemist saw his own *nigredo* as a darkening of the soul, a period when chaos appeared within his experiments, a person in the shadow stage projects inner issues out onto the world and the people in it.

One reason Jung was so convinced of this correspondence was that he found alchemical images appearing in dreams, both his own and those of his patients. Understanding the source of these images helps illuminate what is going on inside the patient at such times. Jungian analyst Edward Edinger has written a major book, *Anatomy of the Psyche*,[13] in which he looks at the major alchemical operations and the alchemical images that represent those operations, then discusses what is going on in the psyche at those times. This knowledge has helped me many times in trying to understand dreams. Note, though, that to fully understand the images one does need to recognize the alchemical stage within which an operation is taking place, as you will read later in this chapter.

You may also recall from the introduction that religious historian Mircea Eliade's interpretation was similar to Jung's, though with a different emphasis. He thought that Jung had the relationship between individuation and the alchemical opus backwards, that individuation was a reenactment of the alchemical opus. Or, more exactly, that "in the very depths of the unconscious, processes occur that bear an astonishing resemblance to the stages in a spiritual operation—gnosis, mysticism, alchemy—which does not occur in the world of profane experience, and which on the contrary, makes a clean break with the profane world."[14] This resemblance is why I have argued that these processes speak to all systems of spiritual transformation. The fact that a similar resemblance also appears in a modern scientific model—chaos theory—is remarkable, as it seems to indicate that the factors generated deep in the psyche of initiates in many different cultures and times also operate similarly in nature. Late in his life, after his joint work with Nobel laureate physicist Wolfgang Pauli, Jung had argued that a *unus mundus*, a unitary world, underlay both matter and psyche. So it seems.

The *Albedo*

We have already stressed that each stage of the alchemical opus was qualitatively different from the stage that preceded it, yet each *emerged* from the previous stage. We will see that this pattern is characteristic of emergence, whether in the psyche or the physical world. At the point when the *albedo* was ready to emerge from the *nigredo*, alchemists reported that they saw scintillae of light shining within the darkness. These sparks of light would appear and disappear, seemingly at random. Jung felt that these sparks were actually "visual illusions" that the alchemists had projected onto "the arcane substance"; that is, they were projecting an inner emergent process out on the experiment they were conducting. This may be so, or it may be that matter itself also evidences the stages of the hermetic transformation process that we find in the alchemical opus, in individuation, and in any tradition that reaches a similar psychological depth. The alchemists might well have actually seen such a process since it is a form of emergence that occurs throughout the physical world in chaotic systems. We will discuss examples of such emergence later in this chapter.

The unconscious mind is ever busy, mixing and remixing, trying out combinations that form for a time like some primitive consciousness that underlies ego-consciousness. Distinctions come into being, then pass back into the chaos as other distinctions emerge in turn. Even if these sparks did actually appear during the experiment, they were also at one and the same time necessarily sparks of new consciousness that were emerging from the unconscious. As Jung said: "One would have to conclude from these alchemical visions that the archetypes have about them a certain effulgence or quasiconsciousness, and that numinosity entails luminosity."[15]

"Numinosity entails luminosity." That's quite a pairing, and one that has appeared in the religions and mythologies of many cultures from the earliest times. Mircea Eliade agrees, saying that "light mystically perceived denotes transcendence of this world . . . It is a certain sign of the revelation of ultimate reality—of reality devoid of all attributes."[16] This was what the alchemists were seeing at this point—*ultimate reality*, which was *devoid of all attributes* because it had not yet emerged into consciousness. Through their experiments, which were not only chemical experiments, but also explorations of their own psyches, they had arrived at a depth of the psyche that transcended ego-consciousness. Something was trying to emerge from the collective into their individual psyches and thus, inevitably, it had a numinous quality. *They saw lights because primitive bits of consciousness were forming within their own psyches!*

Sometimes the alchemical literature uses less literal images than sparks of light to describe this process of emergent order. For example, in a famous fifteenth-century alchemical book, *Aurora Consurgens*, there is instead an image of countries coming together: "For they shall gather me together out of all the countries, that they may pour upon me clean water, and I shall be cleansed . . . ." The late Jungian analyst Marie-Louise von Franz interprets this motif of "gathering together out of all the countries" as "an allusion to the gathering of the 'light particles' or 'soul particles' of God which are scattered throughout matter."[17]

Note that it is "me" that is being gathered, and "me" upon whom the clean water is poured. The image of cleansing is characteristic of the early parts of the *albedo* stage, in which the vestiges of the darkness left from the *nigredo* must be removed through a repetitive cleansing process. The picture in figure 5.2 is another from the Michael Maier series of alchemical pictures. In the epigram that accompanies this picture, Maier says, "Let one who loves to study secret dogmas not fail to take up every helpful hint: You see a woman, washing stains from sheets as usual, by pouring on hot water. Take after her, lest you frustrate your art, for water washes the black body's dirt."[18]

Another image from Maier (figure 5.3) compares the cleansing of the *albedo* stage to a leper cleansing his body to rid it of its illness. "The sick ore of the Wise is swollen up with dropsy, and for healing waters yearns.

Figure 5.2. *Albedo* stage, from *Atalanta fugiens*, epigram 3.

Figure 5.3. *Albedo* stage, *Atalanta fugiens*, epigram 13.

As Naaman shed his leprosy in Jordan,* so thrice and four times by its springs is washed. Therefore precipitate your bodies in fresh water which soon will work to cure them of disease."[19]

Note that both of these instances of *solutio* are far different from the *solutio* that heralds the *nigredo* stage. That *solutio* is a total dissolution of the *prima materia* (and the psyche of the alchemist), leading to the necessary chaos. Now further dissolving is needed in the *albedo*, but only to wash off remaining dirt, or in tougher situations, to cure disease. After shadow issues are worked through, one needs to deal with the issues not merely psychologically, but in real life. Issues are no longer black and white, but have shadings, which create moral difficulties in our lives. We feel dirty and need to cleanse ourselves, but to do so it takes a magical cleansing like that which could heal the leper. Psychologically, this repetitive cleansing corresponds to releasing emotions over and over until everything that we feel is dirty and needs to be hidden has been released. That release of

---

* Naaman was a general from Damascus, Syria, who was cured of his leprosy by bathing seven times in the river Jordan, at the command of the Hebrew prophet Elisha. This story is told in 2 Kings 5.

emotions is characteristic of the anima/animus stage in Jungian psychology. The ability to hold the tension between opposites is especially important during this stage. And no opposite is more apparent than that between male and female, so the need to join the two is the perfect symbol for what has to be accomplished during the *albedo*.

In the previous chapter, you saw pictures from the *Rosarium Philosophorum* that presented the alchemical opus in terms of a joining of the masculine and feminine. The King and Queen went into a pool where they dissolved and joined. From this joined pair, a winged child emerged and rose to the heavens. It later returned to reanimate the now-hermaphroditic figure and complete the opus. In Maier, however, we find images of the hermaphroditic figure near the end of the *albedo* stage having to undergo a further heating (*calcinatio*) to drive away impure elements left after the joining (figure 5.4). Maier describes the figure thus: "Twofold in head and sex, just like a corpse it looks, after its moisture is removed. Hidden in darkest night, it needs the fire: Give it this, and it comes at once to life. The fire conceals the stone's power; in the gold is Sulphur's, in the silver, Mercury."[20] The figure is purified and reanimated through this process of slow heating.

Figure 5.4. *Albedo* stage, *Atalanta fugiens*, epigram 33.

Note again that this *calcinatio* is quite different from the heating during the *nigredo* stage, in which heating is necessary to help fully dissolve the *prima materia*. Now a dry heating is needed not to dissolve, but to drive off remaining moisture. To again quote Morienus the hermit: "The whole key to accomplishment of this operation is in the fire, with which the minerals are prepared and the bad spirits held back, and with which the spirit and body are joined. Fire is the true test of this entire matter."[21]

The alchemist has reached the final part of the *albedo* stage, having passed through the darkness of the *nigredo* and emerged with an early glimpse of the numinous light that will eventually form the philosopher's stone in his experiments and new insights in his life. During the *albedo*, repeated cleansing of both the embryonic stone and the alchemist's psyche has occurred. The tension of opposites has been held sufficiently long for new life to form. But when that new life joins with the pairing of opposites, one further step is needed. Because of all the alchemist has accomplished at this point, he will have a tendency to puff up and feel too full of himself. Jungians use the apt word *inflation* for this occurrence. In this state, we are filled with emotion, but it is a false emotion that we don't own. To progress further, a slow process of burning (a *calcinatio*) has to take place, a burning off of that false emotion, leaving us afterward impervious to such identification. Only then, cleansed, whitened, can we bring in the true blood of life.

The *Rubedo*

The *rubedo* is the stage in which the whiteness of the *albedo* slowly becomes infused with blood and the adept becomes truly alive. All the earlier insights have to be merged into the realities of the world we live in. If Eliade is right and all spiritual paths must necessarily encounter the same alchemical levels of the psyche, we would expect to find this same insight in all cultures.

In Zen Buddhism, there is a famous series of ten drawings from the twelfth century called "In Search of His Missing Ox" that describes the stages of this process. The missing ox represents our essential nature, the philosopher's stone, so to speak, contained within each of us. We must lose that identity with our essential nature in the *nigredo* stage, find it again in the *albedo* stage, then bring it back into the world in the *rubedo* stage. In the first of the Buddhist pictures (figure 5.5), a young man is searching for his missing ox. Along the way, he briefly spots the ox, then loses sight of it again (like the scintillae of light shimmering in and out of existence). He finally catches the animal, harnesses it,* and brings it back home. This corresponds to gaining control of our inner nature, bringing body and mind into harmony. But this doesn't end the story; there are three further pictures. In the first, the picture simply shows a circle that fills the page. This image could represent the completion of the *albedo* stage. The next shows a stark tree above rocks. This picture would represent how the natural world appears when one begins the *rubedo*. In the final picture, the young ox-herder meets an old, fat, jovial master (figure 5.6). Above their heads is a lovely, leafy tree. At this stage, the end

Figure 5.5. Searching for the missing ox, stage 4.

---

* Cat Stevens's album *Catch Bull at Four* refers to the fourth picture, where the ox-herder once more catches and tames the bull.

Figure 5.6. Searching for the missing ox, stage 10.

of the opus, one has returned to the natural world and found it lovely. Old and young are joined, just as all oppositions are joined within the adept.

Chaos Theory: Chaos and Emergence

Instead of thinking of the whole as the sum of all parts, think of it as what rushes in under the guise of chaos whenever scientists try to separate and measure dynamical systems as if they were composed of parts.

—John Briggs and F. David Peat[22]

There are three essential discoveries of chaos theory:

- Some systems exhibit sensitive dependence on initial conditions; that is, small causes can have large effects.

- Determinism and predictability are not necessarily synonymous.

- In "far-from-equilibrium" systems—ones that are chaotic or at the "edge of chaos"*—change can "emerge" from within.

We have already discussed sensitive dependence on initial conditions in connection with Lorenz's discovery of chaos with his simplified mathematical model of the weather. Though I haven't mentioned it explicitly, this property is also evident in the Mandelbrot set, the logistics map, and strange attractors. The second discovery, that determinism and predictability are not synonymous if there is feedback, is also clear in all those examples. You may recall Lorenz's comment that "I realized that any physical system that behaved nonperiodically would be unpredictable." We are going to discuss this second discovery in more detail next. Afterward, we will discuss the third discovery: emergence.

Deterministic Chaos

The popular idea of chaos is confusion and disorder. In contrast, as we saw earlier in this chapter, the alchemists realized that because chaos was undifferentiated, it contained all possibilities within itself; order was hiding away within the confusion. This profound idea is echoed by chaos theory. Before chaos theory, any such idea would have been considered ridiculous in science. In general, when scientists, no matter what their specialized field, look at the world around them, they assume that there is an order and it is their task to discover that order. To use a phrase poet Wallace Stevens used for writers, they have a "rage for order."[23] There is also an implicit belief that the order they discover can be reduced to a finite set of laws and rules that lead to predictable, measurable results. When experimental results don't fully conform to their predictions, the assumption prior to chaos theory was that these differences were due to experimental error.

---

* *The edge of chaos* is a popular term used especially by those in complexity theory (a close cousin of chaos theory). It means that a system is at a level of complexity in which order is still present, but any little push can move it into chaos.

Chapter Five

In the late days of the nineteenth century, philosopher and logician Bertrand Russell used to give a lecture in which he described how biology and chemistry could be reduced to physics; physics could be reduced to mathematics; and mathematics to logic. Proving the last part was for Russell the most important piece in the puzzle. He had been working on it with only minor success when, in September 1900, he heard Giuseppe Peano, an Italian mathematician and logician, present an elegant mathematical formalism in which the entire set of natural numbers (i.e., 1, 2, 3, . . .) could be produced by using only five axioms.* Russell was captivated by Peano's system and immediately decided it provided the missing elements he needed to prove that mathematics (or at least number theory and set theory, which are the core of mathematics) could be reduced to logic. He considered proofs that the sciences could be reduced to mathematics to be of lesser importance, which could later be accomplished by others. Russell commented that "the time was one of intellectual intoxication. My sensations resembled those one has after climbing a mountain in a mist, when, on reaching the summit, the mist suddenly clears, and the country becomes visible for forty miles in every direction . . . Intellectually the month of September 1900 was the highest point of my life."[24]

Together with his older colleague, philosopher Alfred North Whitehead, Russell worked on this project for ten years. The final product ran to more than 4,500 manuscript pages; Russell had to hire a workman to carry the manuscript to the publisher in a cart. The published book, *Principia Mathematica*, was in three volumes and more than 2,000 pages long. And yet it didn't accomplish its goal; Russell was beaten by a tiny paradox inherent in logic itself. In this case, paradox means a statement whose truth or falsity cannot be determined. Russell was aware of this paradox even before he started the project, as he had pointed to the same problem in the work of logician Friedrich Frege. But with the confidence

---

* Axioms are "self-evident" assumptions from which any system is developed. In mathematics, the truth or falsity of axioms is not examined, just what can be derived logically if the axioms are accepted. When I was majoring in mathematics in college I took a course in which we developed the real numbers and some of their properties using Peano's axioms.

of a young man (Russell was twenty-eight when he started the project), he was confident that the paradox would soon yield to analysis. When it stubbornly remained intractable, Russell tried to sidestep the problem by constructing a convoluted "system of types." The complexity caused by this solution was one reason *Principia* was so long. He thought that his approach resolved the paradox. In 1931, however, mathematician and logician Kurt Gödel went the other way and approached the paradox head-on. That tactic worked, and it produced a result that many regard as the most important intellectual accomplishment of the twentieth century. Very carefully building up the paradox within mathematics itself, Gödel initially proved that Russell's system and any similar system necessarily contain statements whose truth or falsity cannot be demonstrated with the system. And if you try to get around that problem by assuming that the axioms used in the system can never lead to such results, then Gödel proved there are true statements in the system that cannot be derived from the axioms. He went on to extend his proof to include any nontrivial formal system (which means not only all of mathematics, but also all of science).[25]

Like most of us, mathematicians tend to be pragmatists. Even if they acknowledged that Gödel had proved there were limits to what they could do, they assumed that those limits were probably only encountered in exceptional cases; they would continue on with what they were doing. Most scientists were not even aware that Gödel had proved their ultimate goals to be impossible; they had other worries. In the early part of the twentieth century, well before the younger Gödel presented his shocking proof, Einstein produced his twin theories of relativity. At much the same time came the discoveries of quantum mechanics. Suddenly the world was becoming much less clear and predictable. But still there was an assurance that order prevailed in nature and certainly in the applied mathematics used to predict nature's behavior, despite Gödel's proof. Then came chaos theory. What was initially so startling about chaos theory was the realization that simple equations, such as those Lorenz used, could lead to unpredictable results when the results were fed back into the equations at each stage. Suddenly results that had been dismissed as experimental errors were seen to be products of the inherent unpredictability of even deterministic equations.

What does this term *deterministic* mean? It simply means a problem can be solved in a step-by-step way in which each step depends only on the step that preceded it. Lorenz's formulas, for example, start with a small number of equations and an initial set of values to be fed into the equations. Each time, the resulting set of values is fed back into the equations and new values calculated. This method contrasts with one involving backtracking, where at each step there may be several possible actions and no way to chose among them except by trying each one and, if it fails, going back and trying another. In general, scientists start with data and try out possible hypotheses to see whether they can reproduce the data. Mostly they don't succeed at first, so they have to backtrack and try again. Eventually they come up with a hypothesis that they accept so that they can calculate results by using strictly deterministic equations. In his small but significant book, *In the Wake of Chaos*, philosopher of science Stephen H. Kellert writes that "we once thought that a deterministic system and a predictable system were two names for the same thing."[26] But chaos theory now revealed that even deterministic equations can lead to unpredictable results.

What are scientists to do, then? Well, they shift ground. For example, Lorenz's program was an attempt to predict the weather on a computer by using a small number of deterministic equations. In our day, the computers have improved vastly and the mathematical models are more sophisticated. Weather satellites provide scientists with a wealth of data about all the conditions affecting the weather in real time. By using these data, it is relatively easy to predict the weather for the next day or two with a fair degree of certainty. But when the scientists try to predict for longer periods, they run into problems with any model they use. Beyond about a week, the errors grow unacceptably large. And there is no way to get around this problem: chaos is too deeply embedded in the web and weave of nature.[27]

Emergence

In almost any era of modern history, philosophers look to the cutting-edge science of their time to provide a model for the human brain/mind. Sometimes that tendency leads to strange results, as when in the seventeenth century, mathematician and philosopher René Descartes turned to hydraulics to explain the workings of the brain: "Sensory stimulation produced a flux of the animal spirits contained in the heart and arteries. The heart then pushed the spirits into the cerebral cavities, much as the pumps of an organ push air into its pipes . . . After death the brain collapsed and fluid could no longer circulate."[28] Though this description now sounds strange to us, it is more difficult to see the problems when it is our own cutting-edge science that is used as the metaphor. For example, in our time, cognitive psychology uses the computer as a metaphor for the relationship between the brain and the mind, with the brain being the hardware and the mind the software. While at best a useful metaphor, it is hopelessly unsuitable as a model for the actual complexity of the brain/mind.

Drawing on contemporary science for a metaphor can, however, lead to prescient results. By the mid-eighteenth century, the deeper philosophic side of alchemy had largely died, while the technical aspects had begun to evolve into the new scientific field of chemistry. By the early nineteenth century, chemistry had evolved further into a practical science. Chemistry presented philosophers with a metaphysical problem that was not apparent previously in science: chemical compounds are more than the sum of their parts. How is it that a chemical *reaction* can yield a chemical *compound* that has a different composition and properties than the substances that went into the reaction?* It was natural, therefore, for philosopher (and former child prodigy) John Stuart Mill,† writing in the middle of the nineteenth century, to turn to chemistry for an explanatory principle for

---

* It was noticing just such reactions in their experiments that led alchemists to believe that the transmutation of elements—for example, lead to gold—was possible.

† John Stuart Mill was, as mentioned in the discussion of Norbert Wiener in chapter 3, a child prodigy. Both had fathers who were determined to make geniuses out of precocious boys by isolating them from other children and teaching them advanced studies. Both grew to geniuses as adults, but at the expense of emotional difficulties.

the creativity of the mind. In the seventeenth century, philosopher John Locke had presented a view of the mind as a *tabula rasa*, or blank slate, that passively accepted sensory data. In that view, what we term ideas are merely organizations and rearrangements of those data. There are no really new ideas, just rearrangements of sensory data or of ideas that are themselves rearrangements of sensory data. This view still prevailed nearly two centuries later, when Mill considered the issue. In contrast, Mill argued that the mind is capable of combining existing ideas into a *creative synthesis* in much the same way that chemical reactions produce new compounds. In Mill's words:

> When many impressions or ideas are operating in the mind together, there sometimes takes place a process of a similar kind to chemical combination . . . those ideas sometimes melt and coalesce into one another, and appear not several ideas but one . . . [T]he Complex Idea, formed by the blending together of several simpler ones, should . . . be said to *result from*, or be *generated by*, the simple ideas, not to *consist of* them.[29]

By 1875, English philosopher G. H. Lewes drew on Mill's idea of creative synthesis and generalized the idea further, as something that wasn't limited just to chemistry or the mind, but was a general situation throughout nature. Lewes was the first to present a general idea of *emergence*, in a form that is quite similar to views today in chaos and complexity theory:

> Although each effect is the result of its components, we cannot always trace the steps of the process, so as to see in the product the mode of operation of each factor. In the latter case, I propose to call the effect *emergent*. It arises out of the combined agencies, but in a form which does not display the agents in action . . . Every *resultant* is either a sum or a difference of the co-operant forces . . . and is clearly traceable to its components . . . the emergent . . . *cannot be reduced to their sum or their difference*.[30]

All that is necessary to bring Lewes' concept up-to-date are the ideas of *self-organization* and *complex systems*; for example, current chaos theorist Jeffrey Goldstein, whose specialty is emergence, defines *emergence* as "the arising of novel and coherent structures, patterns, and properties during the process of self-organization in complex systems."[31]

We discussed complex systems in chapters 1 and 2 but haven't yet encountered the term *self-organization*. In brief, self-organization means that systems, especially complex systems, tend to get progressively more complex, without any outside intervention. This idea appeared as long ago as the Greek thinkers, but only fully emerged (so to speak!) in the second half of the twentieth century. The term *self-organized* was coined by British psychiatrist, neuroscientist, and mathematician H. Ross Ashby in 1947.[32] A year later, in a short, easily understandable article, American mathematician and scientist Warren Weaver pointed out that traditional science had been hugely successful in areas where only a few variables had to be considered. "Physical science before 1900 was largely concerned with two-variable *problems of simplicity*,"[33] whereas "living things are more likely to present situations in which a half-dozen, or even several dozen quantities are all varying simultaneously, and in *subtly interconnected ways*" [my emphasis].[34] He referred to the problems created by complex systems as those of *"organized complexity,"* and said that these were "all problems which involve dealing simultaneously with a *sizable number of factors which are interrelated into an organic whole.*"[35]

With the development of chaos theory, it became clear that problems of organized complexity were not limited to biology and its treatment of living things. In some complex systems, there might be not dozens of variables, but hundreds, or even thousands. Lorenz's work made scientists realize that complex systems were everywhere. The "problems of simplicity" Weaver had discussed were the tip of the iceberg; "organized complexity" was the rule, not the exception. We have already seen three superb examples of emergence produced by the effects of feedback on simple mathematical equations: the Mandelbrot set in chapter 2 and the logistics map and strange attractors in chapter 4. In the logistics map in particular we see how a beginning structure gradually leads to chaos, which in turn contains new structure. To illustrate this behavior in a little more detail, I'm going to reproduce the logistics map from the previous chapter to make some points I didn't make there (figure 5.7).

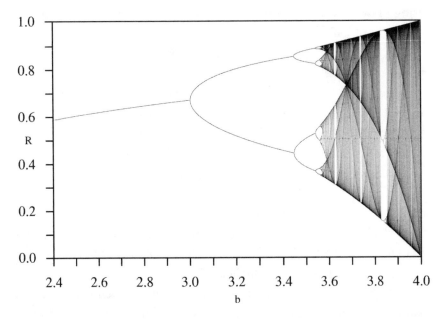

Figure 5.7. Logistics map or bifurcation diagram.

We saw in that chapter that when the birthrate reaches 3.0, the growth pattern bifurcates, so that there are two possible results. At later points, it bifurcates further into four possibilities, then eight, then sixteen, and so forth. On the chart, given the limits of space, you can only see eight bifurcations, but they continue indefinitely before eventually becoming chaotic at a birthrate of 3.57. You can see from looking at the diagram that the difference between one birthrate and the next becomes smaller and smaller. The significance of this pattern was recognized by one of the pioneers of the mathematics of chaos theory, Mitchell Feigenbaum. To see what's happening, let's forget that we're dealing with birthrates and simply take a very, very accurate ruler and measure the distances between bifurcations. We'll call them distance1, distance2, distance3, and so on. If we divide distance1 by distance2, and distance2 by distance3, in each case, we get a ratio. If we continue calculating those ratios, they begin to get closer and closer, until they approach a number called the Feigenbaum constant, which is the infinite number 4.6692. . . . This number doesn't just hold true for the logistics map. It holds for any system that approaches chaos through period-doubling bifurcations. And it appears to hold true not only in the mathematical models of nature, but also in nature itself. This number is as ubiquitous in mathematics and nature as that more famous infinite number, pi. Chaos does have structure!

You may recall that I mentioned earlier in this chapter that alchemists saw scintillae of light appearing in the darkness, as the *nigredo* stage gave way to the *albedo* stage. The sparks of light would appear at random and only gradually coalesce. This pattern of development is typical of emergence in many situations analyzed by chaos theory: the beginnings of new structure appear, then disappear. Only gradually and at no predetermined place or time does the new structure fully form. One example everyone is familiar with is boiling water. The old expression "a watched pot never boils" captures how slowly and unpredictably water comes to a boil. If we do watch the water, we'll see that for a long time, it simply preserves its original structure as water. Then as it approaches the boiling point, little eddies form at different locations in the water, appearing only for a moment, then fading back into the face of the water. At first only a few will appear, scattered widely over the surface. As more time passes and the water further heats, the number of eddies and the rate at which they appear both increase. Some will group together, almost starting the whole pot boiling, but then fade back again. Then at some point—again, I stress, at an unpredictable point—enough of the little whirlpools will come together into a large eddy, which will then seem to suck the rest of the water into itself. At that point the whole surface of the water will seem to be busily boiling. This is truly chaotic, yet a new structure is emerging: steam, the gaseous state of water.

This concept of small individual pieces suddenly combining to form something new is the essential idea of emergence. In his book *The Philosopher's Stone*, physicist and seminal thinker F. David Peat provides an unappetizing but wonderful example from nature: slime mold! Initially slime molds grow from spores into one-celled organisms—amoebas—that feed off microorganisms in decaying vegetable matter, such as that found on the matted floor of forests or even in your backyard. One variety—*Dictyostelida*—has a very special ability. When the food runs out, the amoebas release signal molecules into the air, which causes many amoebas to gather together. When their numbers are sufficient, they give up their individual life and join to form a slug-like creature, which moves to an area where there is more food, much as some higher level animal would do. At that point, the slug stays in place and transforms again into something like a mushroom. During this process, some of the amoebas revert to their original condition as spores while others give up their life to become stalks that push a cap of the spores upwards, where wind can take them, so that they can form anew in still another location.[36]

To move beyond our simple example, consider large-scale but similar changes of structure that pass through chaos to new structure. For example, in weather, picture the sudden formation of a tornado or a hurricane. In the insect world, think of bees in a hive or ants in an ant colony. An individual bee is such a simple creature that its possibilities for action are limited. Yet as enough bees come together in a hive, their interactions lead to emergent phenomena in which large groups of bees act like a single organism. What's more, they do so without any leader to tell them what to do. Yes, there is a queen and she rules the hive, but the functions of the various bees need no direction. The way birds flock together when flying in formation is another beautiful example from nature. No single bird leads the formation; rather the formation moves as a whole. The same is true for schools of fish or even herds of higher animals such as bison. And in group situations, humans also follow their companions into such *emergent behavior*, that is, behavior characteristic of the group, not of the individuals within the group. Consider spectators cheering at a football game or, to pick a less positive example, a crowd responding to a demagogue. The rises and falls of the stock market reflect group activity that is largely independent of individual decision-making processes, especially at extreme periods of a bull or bear market.

Think, too, of the creative process as it operates within us in problem solving. We chew over a problem, endlessly looking at various possibilities, trying this, trying that. Often then we need a period of gestation when the issue drops down into the unconscious, where undoubtedly it continues to be chewed over, though now with possibilities unavailable to consciousness. Then suddenly, at no particular moment, the new insight emerges.

LESSONS FOR SELF-TRANSFORMATION

Since the alchemist's inner journey is so connected with the outer progress of the opus (more on this in the next chapter), we have already discussed some of the implications for self-transformation in discussing the three alchemical stages and how the alchemist is affected. Let's see how those lessons and the lessons from chaos theory turn up in our own lives.

In the alchemical opus, we saw that the *nigredo* stage is characterized by an inner darkness, confusion, and depression; it is the chaos stage of the alchemical journey. Eventually the confusion disappears, the darkness recedes, depression ends, and the *albedo* stage begins. Some people confuse sadness with depression, but depression is not an emotion; it is the absence of the ability to feel emotion. In the *albedo* stage, with the depression gone, actual emotions appear, often accompanied by tears. Our job during this stage is to clean away the remaining darkness; often we are confronted with moral difficulties that cannot be resolved intellectually, only emotionally. Finally, fully cleansed, there is a temptation to remain a hermit, isolated in our inner wisdom. But the opus requires more for us all; we have to return to the world and integrate our personal journey into the normal run of life. This is the *rubedo* stage.

In the previous chapter, I discussed my own experience of being cut into pieces, a process that began my own *nigredo* stage. For many of us, the feeling is more like a related alchemical operation that we only touched on there: the experience of being dissolved into our constituent parts in a *solutio*. In that chapter, I noted that the entire alchemical opus was often summarized as "dissolve and coagulate." The personal experience of dissolution is more gradual than that of being cut apart. My own experience of being cut apart was triggered by a single event. But more commonly, the meaning of our life seems slowly to dissolve, leaving us with less and less to hold on to. Eventually it's as if we have been left in the ocean, trying desperately to stay afloat.

The alchemist experienced this desperation when his experiment came to naught and the literature he depended on for guidance seemed beyond comprehension. Our experience is similar: what once was sure and stable in our lives now fades away. Our marriage, our job, our spiritual values, all lose their appeal. We begin to doubt and that doubt grows, leaving us seemingly alone in the dark. Whether we come to that point gradually or in one fell swoop, from then on, we're all in the same darkness. Again I'll turn to my own experience, since in its outlines it is a universal one. I'll take up the story at the point where I left it in the last chapter.

After my friend was fired, I had fallen into a deep depression. During that time, little lights flickered in the darkness, as I discovered first meditation, then the *I Ching*, the Chinese system of reflection and divination. Both helped a great deal, but it was when I entered a Jungian analysis that I began to slowly find the meaning I had lost in my life. While in analysis, and while still working as an executive, I went back to university to work on a doctorate in clinical psychology, with the goal of becoming a Jungian analyst. Two and a half years after my friend was fired, I felt like I was on the right path again in my life. At that point, it was I who was fired. If my attention had been more on my career, as it had been before, I would have seen it coming. A highly ambitious and unscrupulous higher executive had come into the company and was responsible for a whole line of business, including my area. He gradually fired everyone in management who had been there before. In most cases, the dismissal was not because of incompetence, but because it furthered his own ends. For example, the company had a small department that analyzed the workflow in other departments and made suggestions for improvements. The executive decided he could make a short-term profit by eliminating the department; he didn't care what would happen in the long run, as by then he would have moved up to a still higher position, and workflow would be someone else's problem. He had already cut the department down to one person, the manager, who had been with the company his whole career and was competent at his job. This man was desperately trying to hold on to his job, not realizing, as the rest of us already did, that the executive had already decided to fire him and was just keeping him around a little longer for his amusement. At meetings, the executive played with him like a cat plays with a mouse, taunting him and making him look stupid just for the fun of watching him squirm. And then when the executive finally grew bored, he fired him.

So I should have realized that eventually I would be fired, too, but I didn't, largely because the executive had made so many promises to me. But, to be honest, while I was still doing acceptable work, my heart wasn't in the job any more. I was already looking to the future and that future was as a psychologist, not an executive. The firing came at the hands of someone I liked, someone who went out of his way to make sure that I received a golden parachute from the company: six months of full salary to make a transition to a new position. A few days after I was fired, I received an offer from a major consulting firm to take a position at a similar level with them at a slightly higher salary. I wasn't even tempted; I had come far enough on the new path to know I couldn't go back. But six months later, when the money ran out, my course didn't seem so clear. I was still several years away from my doctorate, with no prospect of income in sight until then. The money situation got desperate: we were overdue on all our bills; the bank threatened foreclosure on our home. My wife sold an upright player piano and anything else she could find, but that was just a drop in the bucket. What she did do that helped me survive was tell me, "I've been poor before and I can be poor again. I'll live in a cardboard box as long as I can live with you."

I felt trapped; it seemed that the only way to make money again was to return to being an executive in computer work. To me at the time, that meant that the whole journey I had taken was meaningless. Doesn't this sound like the alchemist's position in the *nigredo* stage? At that point, I received a job offer that I could accept. In the best full-circle fashion, the friend whose own firing had started my journey was responsible for getting me that job offer. The firing that had shattered my life wasn't nearly so traumatic for my friend, as he knew he was in over his head. He took a job programming for an actuarial consulting firm. I had forgotten, yes forgotten, that I had another marketable skill. Earlier in my career, I had become an associate of the Society of Actuaries (which is the equivalent of a master's degree in actuarial science; the doctoral equivalent is a fellow of the Society). But I had long since dropped actuarial work when I found computers more interesting. The actuarial consulting firm offered me a position in which I didn't have to be an employee; I could be a consultant to the firm itself, setting my own hours so I could work as much or as little as I wanted and bill them on an hourly basis. I settled on three days a week and continued to see patients and work on my doctorate the rest of the time. Money was still tight, but gradually the situation became manageable.

I think my story shows the complexity of how the alchemical stages of *nigredo*, *albedo*, and *rubedo* actually evidence themselves in life. My friend's firing dropped me into the chaos and depression of the *nigredo* and left me there to thrash about. I worked my way through that period and came to a whitening, a clarity, due to the combination of meditation, the *I Ching*, and a Jungian analysis. But that wasn't sufficient for my new insights to survive in the outer world. I found myself in a moral dilemma, pulled between the desire to hold onto my executive status and my need to leave it behind and become a Jungian analyst. Since I couldn't resolve the issue on my own, life resolved it for me by having me fired. At least I was brave enough not to accept the immediate job offer. But I wasn't very realistic about my financial position. I felt that because I was following the path intended for me everything would automatically take care of itself. And in fact it did, but not without my having to struggle more, out of money and not knowing how to pay the bills. Again isn't that reminiscent of the last stages of the *albedo*, when one is stretched out on a rack with a fire burning underneath to get rid of the last "moisture" remaining? The new work arrangement, which offered a balance between earning money and helping others, began the *rubedo* stage for me. The path I then followed was long and complex, but the new stage had at least begun. I'll mention a much earlier personal experience in the next chapter, but first a few more words more on what we learned from chaos theory.

The shocking discovery of chaos theory was that equations could be followed in a step-by-step process, yet at some undetermined point, things could change dramatically with no outside intervention. Things could even become chaotic. I think we see this situation over and over in psychological change. Our lives are following a known course whose endpoint seems, if not predetermined, at least likely. That was the course my life was on before my friend was fired, and then everything changed in a moment. That's the way it can be: life's going down a very predictable path, then something out of nowhere changes everything, and we don't even understand why. What really happens is that beneath the surface tiny differences have accumulated, little dissatisfactions perhaps with our life. But we aren't aware of them. Then, just as the butterfly effect says that the flutter of a butterfly's wings in Brazil can set off a tornado in Texas, those tiny changes can sometime lead to chaotic changes in our life, as in my own story. But chaos theory also shows that the new order "emerges" out of the chaos in a way that couldn't be predicted in advance. If this change occurs even in a computer model with simple algorithms, isn't it much more likely that something new can emerge within the complexity of a human life?

~Chaos and Emergence~

6

The Philosopher's Stone

No one can excel in the alchemical art without knowing the principles in himself, and the greater the knowledge of the self, the greater will be the magnetic power attained thereby and the greater the works to be realized.

—Cornelius Agrippa

In alchemy, from its earliest beginnings, writers stressed that the alchemist had to be pure of heart and conduct his experiments for the glory of God, not for personal gain. The earlier alchemists were not yet aware that their own progress actually paralleled the progress of the alchemical opus; only over time did this realization slowly develop. By the seventeenth century, however, many alchemical writers had come to understand that the true purpose of the alchemical opus was actually the development of the alchemist's soul. It was at just this point that alchemy began to die and science to emerge. In science, a new philosopher's stone was sought: Instead of hastening the processes of Nature (with a capital "N"), the goal became mastery of nature (with a little "n"). In the process, humanity left the Garden of Eden for a second time. Just at the point when the alchemists had come to realize that the stone they sought was their own transformation, scientists decided that what went on inside them had nothing to do with their task. They needed to be totally separated from the world they sought to understand and control. This new attitude produced many great triumphs over the next three hundred years. But in the twentieth century, holes began to appear in the scientific vision, as it became clear from quantum theory that the observer could never really be separate from the world he observed. The full realization that the goal that scientists are really seeking is their own completion has yet to come. We will see, however, that some recent scientific discoveries point in that direction, and chaos theory and related fields (such as complexity theory, catastrophe theory, cybernetics, systems theory, and a wide variety of others that are often lumped together under the general term *nonlinear dynamics*) are at the cusp of this deeper understanding of reality.

ALCHEMY

The ... Philosopher's Stone ... is beyond the comprehension of the uninitiated, though children may play with it or servants throw it into the street; although it is everywhere, it is also the most elusive of things.

—Mircea Eliade[1]

Alchemical Gold: Health, Wealth, and Eternal Life

The philosopher's stone had three miraculous abilities. It could transform lower metals such as lead into gold, which was considered the purest metal; it could cure all illness; and it could provide eternal life.

Gold was considered pure and incorruptible; unlike other metals, gold never tarnishes, because it is an inert metal that does not react with most chemicals. When gold was separated from an amalgam of gold and mercury, it seemed to the alchemist as if part of the mercury had been transformed into gold. In chapter 4, we described how mercury was itself most commonly produced by intensely heating cinnabar to break it apart into mercury and sulphur; this change was symbolically expressed by the separation of the King and Queen who had been joined together in earlier operations. So to the alchemists, it seemed a quite natural progression from cinnabar to mercury, which itself only became gold depending on the right combination with sulphur. Remember that the alchemists felt that they were speeding up the natural processes that took place within the bowels of the earth, where the cruder metals grew like living organisms, becoming ever more pure until they eventually became gold. Ores and metals were regarded as alive: one spoke in terms of their gestation, growth, birth, and even marriage. Beyond this understanding, which alchemists shared with the metallurgical mystery guilds, was the further idea that this task was equally a spiritual one:

> The alchemists adopted and gave new significance to these primitive beliefs. The alchemical combination of sulphur and mercury is always expressed in terms of "marriage." But this marriage is also a mystical union between two cosmological principles. Herein lies the novelty of the alchemical perspectives: the life of Matter is no longer designated in terms of "vital" hierophanies as it was in the outlook of primitive man; it has acquired a spiritual dimension.[2]

Gold's beautiful color led to its association with the sun from ancient times. Since the sun brought light and its absence darkness, early civilizations worshiped it. In addition to its beautiful color, gold is solid and heavy, yet soft enough to be worked fairly easily by metalworkers. It is malleable enough that it can be beaten and stretched almost without limit; for example, a single ounce can be beaten into a square sheet measuring more than fifteen feet on each side. Because of these qualities, gold was in general the most highly valued of all metals. It was also believed that contact with gold could preserve health; after all, if gold were itself pure and incorruptible, it was only reasonable to believe that exposure to gold could transfer those qualities, improving one's health.

Gold has also become particularly associated with wedding rings. We know of wedding rings being exchanged in Egypt almost five thousand years ago. Though these first rings were of woven rushes and weeds, when metallurgy developed, a variety of metals came to be used, including iron, silver, and gold. Gold became the metal of choice in many cultures, in part because of its expense, so that it could serve as an outward sign of the worth of the bride to the groom. Because of gold's purity and incorruptibility, it also served as a visible expression of fidelity to the spouse. And because of its association with health, it was believed that it could keep both the wearer and the marriage healthy.

If gold could keep someone healthy, how much more potent would be the *lapis*, since the *lapis* could itself change lower metals to gold. Eliade points out that "Arabian alchemists were the first to ascribe therapeutic properties to the Stone, and it was through Arabian alchemy that the conception . . . came to the West." In the thirteenth century, physician and alchemist Arnold of Villanova quantified just how effective the *lapis* was in curing illness, concluding with the attribution of something akin to eternal life. He wrote that "the Philosopher's Stone cures all maladies. In one day it cures a malady which would last a month, in twelve days a sickness which would last a year, and a longer one in a month. It restores youth to the old."[3] Health, wealth, and eternal life through the production of the philosopher's stone!

Nicholas Flamel

We can hardly write about the philosopher's stone without mentioning the legendary fourteenth-century Parisian alchemist Nicolas Flamel, who was reputed to have produced the philosopher's stone (which by this time in history was a magical powder rather than a stone) and used it to produce gold and become rich and powerful. In a volume attributed to Nicolas Flamel, but more likely written well after his death, he says that "this mercury I truly transmuted into almost as much gold, much better, indeed, than common gold, more soft also and more pliable. I speak it in all truth: I have made it three times."[4]

With that wealth, he and his wife Pernelle (whom he regarded as an equal partner in his work) became the most prominent philanthropists of their day, founding, in the words of Flamel from the same disputed document quoted above, "fourteen hospitals, three chapels, and seven churches, in the city of Paris,"[5] as well as a similar number in Boulogne. In addition to these physical displays of their philanthropy, they also provided less publicly for the welfare of widows and orphans. There is supportive outside evidence for this philanthropy, though with all these issues, it's hard to know how to separate fact from fiction.

It is significant that Flamel lived and died in the fourteenth century, a time before the Renaissance enlightenment, a time when miracles and wonders were still taken at face value. In some accounts, Flamel and Pernelle not only used the powder to produce gold, but also to attain immortality. In one of the more unbridled accounts from the seventeenth century, archaeologist Paul Lucas reported that in Turkey he met a philosopher who "was a member of a group of seven philosophers, who belonged to no country and travelled all over the world, having no other aim than the search for wisdom and their own development." These mystical philosophers supposedly lived an average of a thousand years, for each had knowledge of the philosopher's stone, and Flamel was one of the seven! Flamel had faked his and his wife's deaths, creating elaborate funerals. In actuality, he was now living in "India, the country of the initiates."[6] In still another report, this time from the eighteenth century, though Flamel died about 1417 and his wife a few years earlier, they were supposedly seen attending the opera in Paris . . . in 1761!

His story is a fascinating one that has remained alive to this day: he has been mentioned in a number of popular contemporary novels, including Umberto Eco's *Foucault's Pendulum* and Dan Brown's *The Da Vinci Code*. Perhaps most famously of all, in J. K. Rowling's *Harry Potter and the Philosopher's Stone*, Flamel figures as a never-seen character who has lived for hundreds of years because of his discovery of the stone. When the stone was destroyed at the end of the novel, his immortality had to end. Rowling reports on her Web site that Flamel has since died.[7]

There does seem to have been an actual Nicolas Flamel who was born somewhere around 1330 in either Paris or Pontoise. The actual Flamel came from a humble background but had enough education to become a notary or book copier. More importantly for his later success, he also set up shop in his home with a number of apprentices as a book publisher and seller. This was a time when the demand for books was just beginning to grow. He produced a variety of books that were successful and earned him a good reputation. In his marriage to Pernelle, who had been twice widowed, he found a companion who was not only handsome, loving, and practical but also brought a good deal of money to the marriage. She was also an excellent business manager. Since the pair lived thriftily, some of the debunkers of his story have argued that it is easy to see how they grew rich without any need for the philosopher's stone. I won't bother to try to debunk Flamel in this account, since his is clearly a miracle story of a type that abounded in the late Middle Ages.

The story of Flamel as an alchemist has been told in many ways, with many amplifications. In one version, Flamel had a dream in which an angel appeared before him holding a beautiful ancient book. He was told to look closely at the book even though he would not understand its meaning at this time. When he reached for it, the book and the angel disappeared. Various versions then tell how the book of his dreams actually came into his life. The following version appears in one of the many books attributed to Flamel (despite the attributions, none appears to have actually been written before the seventeenth century). One of those books contains the last testament of Nicolas Flamel, supposedly written in 1399, though the first known publisher of the book was P. Arnauld de la Chevalerie in the early seventeenth century.[8] In this testament, Flamel says that in 1357, "there fell by chance into my hands a gilded book, very old and large, which cost me two florins."[9] He immediately recognized it as the book from his dream. It was a very strange book, as the pages were made not of paper or parchment, but of thin bark, twenty-one pages in all. I'll let Flamel continue here:

Tantalus

> Upon the first of the leaves there was written, in large capital letters of gold: "Abraham the Jew, Prince, Priest, Levite, Astrologer, and Philosopher, to the nation of the Jews dispersed by the wrath of god in France, wisheth health."
>
> After which words, it was filled with many execrations and curses, with this word MARANATHA, which was oft repeated against any one that should look in to unfold it, except he were either Priest or Scribe.[10]

The book taught "in plain words, the transmutation of metals," with colored drawings of the alchemical vessels on the margins, to illustrate what should arise at each key point. "But of the *prima materia* or first matter, or agent, he spake not so much as one word."[11] Flamel studied the book endlessly, but without the knowledge of the *prima materia*, he couldn't really begin. He copied the book and took it with him as he wandered for twenty-one years (so the text claims) in search of answers. Finally he met a "Jew by nation, but now a Christian," who knew of the book, but had never seen it before. They became deep friends and voyaged together back to Flamel's home so that his new friend could see the actual book. During the voyage, together they figured out the *"prima materia,* the first principles, but not their first preparation."[12] Unfortunately (or fortunately for the story), his Jewish/Christian friend became deathly ill and died on the voyage. Once home again, now knowing what the *prima materia* was, Flamel set to work to create it; this process took him three more years.

For a clearer understanding of this odd tale, we turn to Patrick J. Smith, a translator and scholar of alchemical texts. In his notes on this text, he comments that "it was typical of medieval alchemical treatises to veil the operations of the Great Work under such an allegorical journey."[13] All the specifics of such a journey were symbolic clues for what happened during the opus. For example, the twenty-one years of his journey undoubtedly referred to the twenty-one leaves of the famous book. Smith points out a reference in this supposedly fourteenth-century narrative to alchemical texts that first appeared in Europe in the seventeenth century, as well as to numerous images that appeared widely in alchemical texts of the late Renaissance and into the seventeenth century. Finally, in considering whether this text was actually by Nicolas Flamel, the reader needs to know that later alchemical writers also often ascribe their text to some legendary alchemical figure, from Hermes Trismegistus to Flamel himself.

But certain objects indicate not only that Nicolas Flamel actually existed, but also that he regarded himself as an alchemist. For example, "his tombstone is still to be seen along a stairway in Paris's Musée de Cluny."[14] It contains a series of images (figure 6.1) that symbolize stages of the alchemical opus and that were supposedly taken from the famous book.

Figure 6.1. Alchemical images on Nicolas Flamel's tombstone.

Over and beyond the cottage industry in legends of Flamel's life, other stories appeared purporting to explain what happened to the famous book after Flamel's death (these stories assume that he died). The most often told version is that it passed, along with his other papers and perhaps the magical powder, to a nephew named Perrier, and from Perrier on from father to son within the family for two centuries, eventually ending up in the hands of a seventeenth-century descendent named Dubois. Dubois supposedly possessed a small amount of the powder and used it to produce gold for the king. As kings are wont to do, he wanted more, according to the tale. His chief minister, Cardinal Richelieu, tried to persuade Dubois to reveal the secrets so that he could himself produce the powder. Dubois, however, knew only how to use the powder, not how to produce it, and he had no more powder. Tiring of his useless enquiries, Richelieu persuaded the king to have Dubois killed and himself took possession of the book. He had an alchemical laboratory built in his own palace and between his other labors would try to ferret out the secrets of the philosopher's stone, but to no avail. After Richelieu's death, no one knows what happened to the book. As might be expected with such a famous story, a variety of supposed copies of the book were produced. "There are innumerable other stories, from the sixteenth through the eighteenth centuries, of alchemists, or the beneficiaries of alchemists, taking from their pockets little boxes containing things that look like "tiny splinters of fiery red glass" and using them to transform matter into gold. Then that tradition ends."[15] But none of these stories is so often repeated as that of Nicolas Flamel.

Flamel's story seems to echo the idea that the opus had to take place simultaneously both in the alchemist and in the laboratory. His first information came from a dream: from within the alchemist. He had to struggle with the dream material to no avail for some time, but then the book of the dream appeared in the outer world. This event indicated that the inner and the outer worlds were clearly conjoined. But though the book was clear about how to create the philosopher's stone, it did not explain the *prima materia*, the starting point, the basic principles on which all else depended. Flamel had to search on his own for twenty-one years (i.e., through all twenty-one of the leaves of the book) to try to find it. This search is very reminiscent of the notion of the grail quest, which dates back to the late twelfth century, the same period when the code of chivalry came into existence. Depth psychologists consider the grail that was sought to be the missing feminine element that had never before been separated from the sexual within men. In the legend, Percevel (also spelled Parsifal or Parzival and other variants), like Flamel, had to journey for many years and have many adventures before he discovered the grail, which in some sense had always been within him. The parallel is further fascinating because Flamel's relationship with his wife (who was already forty when he married her) was one in which he regarded her not only with love, but also as his equal partner in everything. This attitude was quite unusual for the time and strongly indicates that Flamel had integrated the feminine element within himself. Finally, once the stone had been created and the gold produced, the pair gave generously to those less fortunate, again a sign that the stone had been created within the alchemist as well as without.

Alchemists like Flamel were trying to discover the deepest secrets of the universe. For them, that meant searching for the building blocks of both matter and psyche, for they saw no clear distinction between the two: there was only the relationship between the experimenter and his experiment. They had to meditate deeply on both their own inner nature and the inner nature of the matter upon which they were experimenting. In many ways this is the most important lesson to be learned: the true philosopher's stone that the alchemist seeks is not only outside him, but also within his own soul. So let us regard Flamel's story as an allegory of someone who succeeds in creating the philosopher's stone, and who, in the process, creates the stone within himself. Because Flamel lived at the end of the Middle Ages, just before the enlightenment of the Renaissance, his story is an apotheosis of the type of miracle story so loved during the Middle Ages. That it has captivated readers into our own time shows that it continues to touch something archetypal within the human psyche. While the ultimate aim of the alchemical opus was the production of the philosopher's stone, the stone wasn't intended to exist in a museum, behind glass, for visitors to see: it not only turns lead into gold but heals all wounds and even provides eternal life. It can do all this because it is life itself, the life that exists only after one has passed through darkness during the *nigredo*, cleansed one's soul in the *albedo*, then returned to the world again in the *rubedo*.

The True Philosopher's Stone

In the introduction, we discussed how nineteenth-century authors Mary Atwood and E. A. Hitchcock came to the realization that the alchemical opus was really the story of the inner transformation of the alchemist. Psychologist Herbert Silberer drew heavily on Hitchcock's interpretations in a first attempt at a psychological study of not only alchemy but also other related areas. C. G. Jung then fully psychologized alchemy, with his interpretation that the opus was a projection of the process of individuation that was going on inside the alchemist. Finally, historian of religion Mircea Eliade acknowledged Jung's great achievement in realizing that the unconscious contains innate processes that are uncannily similar to the stages of any deep spiritual path. But Eliade argued that both alchemy and Jung's concept of individuation were expressions of this same innate process, one that is common to all major paths of spiritual initiation. With that realization, the insights of Hitchcock and Silberer become spiritual gold. We don't have to accept that the alchemists were concealing their true purpose while overtly conducting experiments to create the philosopher's stone, which could convert the *prima materia* into gold. Instead we can examine the alchemist's inner process, which Hitchcock and Silberer present so well, without assuming the alchemists themselves understood that process.

To me, it seems likely that the alchemists' realization of the inner transformation developed very slowly over a long period of time. While it was accepted from the beginning that the alchemist had to be pure of heart and honor God to succeed at his task, through the end of the Middle Ages most of the alchemists still believed only in the physical transformation that took place in the opus. Flamel, whether the real or the storied one, can be seen as the apotheosis of this state of alchemy. As the Middle Ages gave way to the Renaissance and beyond, a degree of understanding of the alchemist's inner transformation appeared more and more frequently in alchemical writers. This isn't to say that there wasn't still full belief by many, if not most, that the physical alchemical opus took place. Rather, these writers took the view that both the outer and the inner had necessarily to be in harmony for the opus to succeed. Only after the death of alchemy itself could writers like Atwood and Hitchcock discard the outer aspect totally. At that point, it was possible for Jung to view the outer opus as a psychological projection of individuation.

As long as we don't have to accept that the alchemists always understood their inner path, we can learn a great deal from Hitchcock and Silberer. Hitchcock has this to say of the alchemist's inner work:

> Those who have never had this experience are apt to decry it as imaginary; but those who enter into it know that they have entered into a higher life, or feel enabled by it to look upon things from a higher point of view . . . To use what may seem a misapplication of language, it is a supernatural birth, *naturally entered upon.*[16]

A supernatural birth, naturally entered upon! What a beautifully profound and singularly apt description of the process of self-transformation, not only in alchemy, but also within any spiritual path. Silberer says similarly: "The initially supernatural resolves itself in nature, or better, Nature is raised to divinity."[17]

Throughout this book, we have seen not only that the end of the opus, the philosopher's stone, is already contained in its beginning, but also that it is the effort of going through the process that creates the stone. "Effort itself, not the object of effort, forms the basis of development. No seeker begins his journey with full knowledge of the goal."[18] In Flamel's story, for example, we see that he was so driven to seek the stone that he cared for little else. But it seems clear that he wasn't driven by the desire for riches; it was the stone itself he sought, an indication that what he actually desired was some completeness within himself. "The desired completion or oneness should be a state of the soul, a condition of being, not of knowing."[19] Once he was successful in creating the stone and had used it to make the purest of gold, he didn't hoard the gold and seek to accumulate more and more wealth like some miser; instead he used it to build hospitals and churches and to help the less fortunate. The further stories that he and his wife also acquired immortality seem a later addition to the story, of the sort that is added to all stories of heroic accomplishment. "There is a great difference between one who seeks what he seeks as an end, and one who seeks it as a means to an end."[20]

Finally, we might be reminded of Paracelsus and his belief that it was love alone that joined the world below with the world above, as reflected in this quote from Hitchcock: "[The alchemists] rely chiefly upon *Love* as working the greatest of wonders, that of a transformation of the *subject* of it into the *object loved*."[21] Isn't this the surest sign of how far someone has advanced on any spiritual path: how kind they are, how much they are capable of love for each and every one that they encounter? The true alchemists weren't drawn by dreams of wealth and power and immortality as much as they were pulled by the love of the divine and the hope of being joined with that divinity.

Isaac Newton:
The Bridge between Old and New

Nature and nature's laws lay hid in night; God said "Let Newton be!" and all was light.
—Alexander Pope's epitaph for Newton[22]

The world of traditional men and women was alive with spirits. Everything had both an inner and an outer connection. There was as yet no awareness of psychological reality as separate from physical reality, so both were conjoined for the alchemist. The miraculous was still possible. If it's difficult to put ourselves into such a mind-set, perhaps an extended quote from Evola will help us understand the difference between the view of the natural world held by traditional societies and its contrast with our modern view:

> Modern civilizations stand on one side and on the other the entirety of all the civilizations that preceded it (for the West, we can put the dividing line at the end of the Middle Ages). At this point the rupture is complete . . . For the great majority of moderns, that means any possibility of understanding the traditional world has been completely lost . . . The hermetico-alchemical tradition forms part of the cycle of pre-modern "traditional" civilization and in order to understand its spirit we need to translate it inwardly from one world to the other . . . Ancient man not only had a different way of thinking and feeling, but also a different way of *perceiving* and *knowing*.[23]

Though the unconscious acceptance of nature as sacred began to die with the end of the Middle Ages, hermetic ideas reemerged in new form in the Western world at the beginning of the Italian Renaissance in the fifteenth century. One major influence, mentioned in chapter 2, was Italian philosopher and astrologer Marsilio Ficino, who translated both Plato and the Hermetica from Greek into Latin. Those ancient ideas would fascinate cutting-edge thinkers (and alchemists) for another three hundred years. As the Renaissance progressed, the more philosophically minded alchemists came to realize that all of the miracles attributed to the *lapis* could actually be inner experiences, culminating in the eternal life that one finds when the soul is reunited with the source from which it came. In the words of novelist Paul Coelho: "Alchemy . . . is about penetrating to the Soul of the World, and discovering the treasure that has been reserved for you."[24]

It is not uncommon for areas of art and culture to reach their apotheosis just as they are giving way to newer models. For example, by the eighteenth century, though baroque music was already regarded as old-fashioned, Johann Sebastian Bach brought this "old-fashioned" form to its culmination, creating music that will live forever. In a similar fashion, in the seventeenth century, when the old view of nature was beginning to be supplanted by the newly emergent field of science, alchemy reached its peak. But science had a new "philosopher's stone" to seek. And one man, Isaac Newton, stood at the pivotal point at which the traditional world and the modern world were juxtaposed. One foot rested in the ancient world of alchemy where nature was still alive, while the other foot rested in the modern world of a dead nature subject to measurement and absolutes. His writings reflect this dichotomy to an astonishing degree. Recall this quote from Newton's alchemical notes, which we saw in chapter 3: "For nature is a perpetuall circulatory worker, generating fluids out of solids, and solids out of liquids, fixed things out of volatile, & volatile out of fixed, subtile out of gross, & gross out of subtile."[25] No better short summary of the alchemical view of reality could be desired. Yet here is a quote from the *Principia*, his famous book that inspired scientists for the next three hundred years: "Absolute space, in its own nature, without relation to anything external remains always similar and immovable. Absolute, true, and mathematical time, in itself, and from its own nature, flows equably without relation to anything external."[26] Here Newton shows himself as the prototype of the modern scientist.

Newton's ideas in science and mathematics changed the Western worldview forever, and his achievements were, in large part, the result of his alchemical approach to reality. Yet, as Eliade noted, "In its spectacular development, 'modern science' has ignored or rejected its hermetic heritage. In other words, the triumph of Newton's mechanics abolished

Newton's own scientific ideal."[27] Newton would not have understood what he had wrought, because "Newton was a mechanist and a mathematician to the core, but he could not believe in a nature without spirit."[28] And spirit was something that science no longer felt it needed.

The modern worldview, a position so necessary to the objective, disinterested stance of science, no longer views humanity as an active participant in a living nature, but rather as a passive observer of a nature filled with "things" separate from the observer. This attitude led in turn to the split of mind and body, which found its first advocate in seventeenth-century philosopher and mathematician René Descartes, who proclaimed "*cogito ergo sum*" (I think, therefore I am). For if our primary role is to be an observer, we are capable of observing ourselves. This powerful realization found full expression in the field of psychology. In the process, though, we have forgotten that this split is an artificial one, that mind and body are part of an inherently unified organism. Nor is it possible for human beings to exist in isolation from the world around them; we are all conjoined parts of a complex unity that includes all the supposed objects of observation. As we have already seen in our discussions of chaos theory and related areas, the "scientific" view of man as observer, separate from all he observes, is giving way to what we might see as a new view of a living nature in which everything is connected, including each of us one to another.

It is hard to overestimate the impact of Isaac Newton's discoveries on the West. With his *Optiks* and *Principia*, Newton seemed to his contemporaries to have explained all of nature: motion, force, gravity, and light. Before Newton, there were speculations; after Newton there were Laws! Both space and time were subsumed within his laws. It was this worldview of fixed laws, laws that seemingly described all of reality, that inspired the next generation of scientists. The search for absolutes, for total understanding and control of the natural world, became the new "philosopher's stone" sought by scientists. Newtonian physics was used to support the deistic view that God had created the world as a perfect machine that then required no further interference from Him. The world was like a clock that had been created, wound up, and then set in place. It was up to humanity to discover first how the clock was built, then the laws by which it ran. These ideals were typified in eighteenth-century mathematician and astronomer Pierre-Simon Laplace's expressed view that a Supreme Intelligence, armed with a knowledge of Newtonian laws of nature and a knowledge of the positions and velocities of all particles in the universe at any moment, could deduce the state of the universe at any time past or present. "All the effects of nature are only the mathematical consequences of a small number of immutable laws."[29]

Laplace's masterpiece was the *Mécanique Céleste*, in which he took on the formidable task of fully explaining the movements of the planets, their effects on the tides, and much more. A famous anecdote is told concerning Napoleon's reaction to the book. Napoleon said to Laplace, "You have written this huge book on the system of the world without once mentioning the author of the universe." Laplace answered, "Sire, I had no need of that hypothesis." When Napoleon reported this exchange to Joseph-Louis Lagrange, an equally great (but more modest) contemporary mathematician, Lagrange responded, "Ah, but it is a fine hypothesis. *It explains so many things.*"[30] Napoleon never forgot; in his last days at St. Helena, he commented that Laplace was a great mathematician but a poor administrator; in contrast, he said that "Lagrange is the lofty pyramid of the mathematical sciences."[31] Laplace's attitude was, however, fairly typical of scientists up until the late twentieth century. And, in a muted form, it is still typical of too many scientists today. But Laplace was deeply wrong.

CHAOS THEORY: *AUTOPOIESIS*

It is in this faith in experimental science and grandiose industrial projects that we must look for the alchemist's dreams.
—Mircea Eliade[32]

The Newtonian world in which Laplace believed so completely is a world of separate material "things." The scientist's job is to explain all the interactions among those "things," just as Newton had done so successfully with his laws of motion and gravity. The smallest of these "things" were called *atoms*. Then early in the twentieth century, discoveries in nuclear physics upset the apple cart. Rather than solid "things," atoms were revealed to contain still smaller particles, separated by enormous relative distances; each atom began to seem like a universe in itself. Then came Einstein with his twin theories of relativity, the first of which demonstrated that the only absolute in our universe was the speed of light—hardly a "thing." The second showed that all motion is relative to the observer. In other words, we can try as hard as we want to be separate from the world we observe, but actually what we observe depends on who is doing the observing. Quantum mechanics then showed that those subatomic particles, which we thought must be the smallest "things," were actually made up of something called *quarks*, and quarks have so little physical reality that they are better understood as mathematical constructions. At the quantum level, which is the lowest level we know of at this point, the appearance and disappearance of subatomic particles is best explained not through the cause and effect of Newtonian physics, but instead by probabilities.

To pick one very important example from quantum mechanics, in 1927, physicist Werner Heisenberg formulated his famous uncertainty principle, which said that it is impossible to know with full accuracy both the position and velocity of a subatomic particle; if we increase the accuracy of measurement of one, the accuracy of measurement of the other is decreased. This concept, while dealing only with measurement, led other physicists to realize that it is impossible to observe any subatomic particle without affecting it in the process of observation. For example, for us to "see" an electron, it must interact with a photon of light, and this interaction will change the movement of the electron. Contemporary physicist John Archibald Wheeler took this to the extreme of speculating that the universe might be pictured as a giant eye looking back at itself. Or maybe it is each of us looking back at ourselves?

Cybernetics, which we discussed in chapter 3, pushed these issues out of the subatomic world into the world of our everyday reality. The world can't readily be reduced to simple cause-and-effect chains; the world is cybernetic, with cause leading to effect, which itself is the cause of some new effect, on and on endlessly. Nature puts bounds on this process so that we have both positive and negative feedback operating in these cybernetic spirals. Finally, chaos theory showed "any level or domain of observation or theory may communicate with others without necessarily going through a linear causal chain."[33] And finally we will discuss *autopoiesis*, which complements chaos theory: while chaos theory explains how unexpected change occurs through the process of feedback, autopoiesis explains how things remain stable in a changing world, also through the process of feedback. All together, these discoveries seem to show that the scientist is inseparable from the world in which he conducts his experiments. It's only one further step (which has yet to be taken) to understand that the ultimate purpose is the scientist's own transformation!

Chaos Theory and the Mind/Body Question

In the seventeenth century, inspired by Newton, philosopher John Locke described the human mind as an empty vessel containing separate and distinct particles called *ideas*. All ideas were either simple or complex. The simple ideas came directly from experience; the complex from the mind operating on simple ideas. All ideas thus came directly or indirectly from experience; experience could be either external sensory experience or internal experience of the mind's own states. Though full of difficulties, Locke's views were representative of the mainstream of thought prior to the twentieth century.

In the twentieth century, behaviorism went even further than Locke. It dismissed the mind as unnecessary to explain behavior. Early in the twentieth century, psychologist John B. Watson developed a stimulus-response model that became known as *behaviorism*. In this model, all behavior is considered to be composed of stimulus-response chains, in which a stimulus leads to a response, which in turn becomes the stimulus for still another response. Both stimulus and response are purely physiological events and hence fully measurable. The mind in between can be safely ignored as, at most, an epiphenomenon. In other words, behavior is simply caused by a sensation from the outer world triggering a built-in response. More complicated behaviors involve longer chains of stimuli and responses, but there is no need for feedback and no need for an intervening mind.

The behaviorist model is simply an insufficient description of the relationship between the individual and the world. In the early 1980s, neuroscientist and chaos theory pioneer Walter J. Freeman and his students conducted research that demonstrated that, in fact, the brain (animal and human) is in some sense independent of the outside world. In his book, *Societies of Brains* (1995), Freeman describes the discovery of sensory "attractors" in the brain:

> This book had its origin in an experimental finding and an insight. First, the finding. I was tracing the path taken by neural activity that accompanied and followed a sensory stimulus in brains of rabbits. I traced it from the sensory receptors into the cerebral cortex and there found that the activity vanished, just like the rabbit down the rabbit hole in 'Alice in Wonderland.' What appeared in place of the stimulus-evoked activity was a new pattern of cortical activity that was created by the rabbit brain.[34]

Freeman and his students found that this discovery held for all the sensory systems. In all cases, once the sensory stimuli hit the brain, they disappeared, and instead information previously stored in the brain appeared. *And that same information could be triggered by different sensory stimuli.* In other words, a variety of sensory experiences can lead to the same attractor, while the same sensory experience can lead to a different attractor at a different time. The brain contains attractors for all sensory experience: sight, sound, smell, and feeling. Freeman concluded that his rabbit could never have any knowledge of the actual world; it knew only the world of its brain. Autopoiesis, a field closely related to chaos theory, has examined exactly this kind of situation.

Autopoiesis

The biologists Humberto Maturana and his student and colleague Francisco Varela coined the term *autopoiesis in 1973*, in an attempt to identify what differentiated a living system, such as a biological cell or tree or a human being, from a nonliving system, such as a mineral or a rock or a mountain.

They felt that the key difference was that living systems continually created themselves from within. According to Varela, "[Autopoietic systems] are systems that, in a loose sense, produce their own identity: they distinguish themselves from their backgrounds."[35] The term *autopoiesis* was aptly chosen, as it derives from the Greek words for "self" and "creation." Hence, an autopoietic system is one that creates itself. And, to this point, the only known natural autopoietic systems are biological systems (though Wiener speculated that it was theoretically possible for cybernetic machines to evolve to a point that included self-creation).

For an autopoietic system to create itself, it has to continually provide information to itself about itself. It is constantly involved in a self-referential loop in which it is feeding back the results of its current state to itself to preserve its integrity as an organism distinct from its environment. Another, slightly complicated way to describe this state is to say that such organisms have "semipermeable membranes" between themselves and their environment. Put more simply, the boundary that preserves an autopoietic system's self-identity allows matter and energy and information to pass in and out. In Varela's beautiful words, written not long before his death in 2001:

> The boundaries of my body are invisible, a floating shield of self-production, unaware of space, concerned only with permanent bonding and unbonding. The self is also an ongoing process every time new feed is ingested, new air is breathed in, or the tissues change with growth and age.[36]

Autopoiesis is a new attempt to answer the age-old question of how each of us grows from a baby to a child to a young adult to an aged adult, yet somehow we retain our identity. The simplest level of an autopoietic system is traditionally considered to be a biological cell. Even a biological cell presents the same problem, however, as the molecules that compose it are continuously dying and being recreated, yet the cell retains its essential identity. Maturana and Varela said that it is this very ability, above all others, that defines a living system. In living systems, all other changes must be subordinated to the preservation of identity.

Autopoiesis is a necessary complement to chaos theory, and both depend on feedback. Chaos theory explains how something can make an abrupt change that can't be readily traced to some external cause. Autopoiesis explains how something can retain its essential identity despite varying external circumstances. In both cases, information is being fed back into the system. Autopoiesis considers how that information enables a living organism to retain an identity despite growing and evolving. Chaos theory considers how a small change in that information can, over time, grow until the organism loses its identity in chaos, as a necessary stage toward change.

Together both explain how inner and outer are inextricably mixed, so that the inner can develop independently of outer change, yet even a small outer change can be internalized and eventually lead to a large inner change. In Jungian psychology, the Greek word *temenos*, meaning an enclosed sacred space, is used to describe the container that therapy sessions provide. Consider that each alchemical stage—*nigredo, albedo, rubedo*—is such a *temenos*, which contains both the alchemist and the alchemical operations. Though a variety of repetitive alchemical operations take place within each stage, all are contained within the boundaries of definition of that stage. The same is true for what goes on within the alchemist. This state is what autopoiesis describes. Then at some critical point, which can't be fully predicted in advance, a major change occurs and a new alchemical stage provides a new *temenos*. What goes on with the *nigredo* is qualitatively different from that within the *albedo*, and likewise between the *albedo* and the *rubedo*. And finally the production of the *lapis* is a still larger, magical, holy transformation. These changes are characteristic of the shifts described by chaos theory. Autopoiesis and chaos theory provide a new, quantifiable way of looking at the process of transformation, both outer and inner. Yet neither can match alchemy in its detailed and beautiful descriptions of all the subtle changes that happen within those frameworks.

Chapter Six

LESSONS FOR SELF-TRANSFORMATION

The realization that the philosopher's stone is contained within each of us is a profound one. As we pointed out, just as that realization began to become apparent to the alchemists, science appeared and relegated this insight to the dustbin with other seemingly primitive ideas. This separation of humanity and nature led in time to a separation of mind and body, which has left many in our time feeling alienated not only from all outer support, but also from themselves as well. Still, we cannot return to the preconscious level where we were one with nature in the same way that plants and animals are one with nature. We need to have a second Newtonian revolution in which we are able to unite our knowledge of science with a belief in the holiness of nature that was Newton's inspiration. We need to realize consciously that we are inextricably linked with the entire natural world. Perhaps it has taken the already perceived effects of global warming to get this point across to us. I wish we could also realize that we are one with each and every person on the earth, whether male or female, or dark or pale of skin, or Christian, Moslem, Jew, Buddhist, Sikh, Baha'i, Shinto, secular, or believer of any other kind.

But the best way to make major changes in the world is by making changes within ourselves. Let us, like Nicolas Flamel, work hard to discover the philosopher's stone that lies within, then use that understanding to help others on their own path. Let us learn that "the final outcome of the work can be summed up in the three words: Union with God."[37]

Let me close this chapter and this book with two stories, one from my youth and one often told by hypnotherapist Milton Erickson. The first illustrates the power each of us possesses by being an autopoietic system composed of other autopoietic systems, living within a universe that is itself an autopoietic system. In autopoietic systems, living systems, the overriding purpose of the system is to preserve its own identity, separate from its environment. And yet, paradoxically enough, while it does this, it manages to change over time.

Robin's Polio

I had personal experience of my body as an autopoietic system when I was six and had poliomyelitis. Though I spent some time in the hospital, there was only a short period when I couldn't walk. That was enough time, however, for the muscles in my legs to atrophy. To restore the muscles, the doctors and nurses used a variety of treatments. For example, I would lie for hours with a heat lamp baking my legs. It was so hot that I'd cover my legs whenever the nurses were out of sight. Later I'd sit with my legs soaking in a warm whirlpool bath. I loved that. I also had to nap every day for several hours on doctors' orders; I kept doing that almost into my teens. But mostly there were exercises, largely against resistance. For example, a nurse would press on the heel of my foot and I would try to press back, preventing her from moving my foot. Or I would try to lift weights with my legs. In the early stages, my muscles had so little strength that my side of the resistance was pretty minimal, but the exercises still helped develop the muscles.

Now we come to the autopoiesis. As a complement to the actual muscle exercises, I was taught to visualize myself lifting the weights or resisting the pressure at the same time I was actually attempting the task. This method was developed by an Australian nurse, Sister Elizabeth Kinney, and became quite well known in the early days of fighting polio, long before attempts to battle cancer with visualization. Since I'm not a good visualizer, my "visualizations" weren't really visual; they were more a kind of kinesthetic imagination, a statement that will, I'm sure, make sense only to the small number of you who experience the world in a similar fashion. But the important thing is that I was feeding information to my body about how I *wanted* my body to be, not how it actually was. At that early point, I couldn't actually resist the pressure on my heel; I couldn't actually lift any weights. But I could visualize that I was doing so. I could feed that image of wholeness back to my body through my psyche, and it had the effect of slowly building up the necessary muscles that had atrophied! Eventually I was cured and could return to normal functioning. Because I had learned this method of visualizing (albeit kinesthetically) at such an early age, I was able later to make use of the technique in other parts of my life.

We discover exactly this sort of autopoiesis when we are involved in the process of self-transformation. The final outcome is in some way contained within us from the beginning. It is inchoate, though, until, with inner work, we slowly become that transformed person. In the process of feeding information back within ourselves, both about who we are at a point in time and about who we need to become, gradually we evolve into that person. None of us is wise enough to consciously determine that final outcome. Rather we have to trust that something wiser than ourselves is somehow also within us, guiding us along the way. Even so, we have to do the work, just as I had to do the work to restore my paralyzed legs.

Next let's consider a story about how one seemingly tiny bifurcation can change one's life entirely. This story illustrates nearly all the insights that we have already studied throughout this book.

Joe's Story

The famed hypnotherapist Milton Erickson loved to tell this story, which he claimed to be true. When Erickson was young, there was a young man in town named Joe (or at least he was Joe whenever Erickson told the story.) Joe was a ne'er-do-well. His whole life had followed a progression that seemed destined to lead him to a bad end. Small crimes committed as a child had grown into progressively larger crimes. As a teenager, he spent time in a juvenile detention center; as a young man, he went to prison. He was hardly a model prisoner: he fought back so hard that he spent much of his prison time in solitary confinement. As soon as he got out of prison and came home, he returned to what he knew best and robbed several stores. It seemed like his life was unraveling faster and faster, with a violent death the most likely outcome. At the point when our story of transformation begins, the local police had not yet discovered these latest crimes.

Joe happened to see a beautiful young woman on the street. Cocky as always, he approached her and asked her if she would go with him to a dance that was coming up that weekend. She looked hard at Joe, perhaps seeing something no one before had seen in him. She said simply: "You can take me if you're a gentleman." Now, on the surface it sounds almost laughable to say that to a young criminal. But the word *gentleman*, coming from this particular young woman at this particular time, must have touched a very deep place in Joe. When the night for the dance arrived and Joe appeared to pick her up, he was dressed like a gentleman, and throughout the evening he behaved like a gentleman. The following week, he returned all the stolen goods to their owners, who were so shocked that they didn't report the crimes. Joe approached the girl's father, who was a well-to-do farmer, and asked him for a job. Now either the father could also see something in Joe, or perhaps his daughter talked him into giving Joe a chance. In any case, Joe was hired and worked hard. Gradually a new Joe began to emerge, one that the town came slowly to trust. He and the girl married, ran the farm after her father died, and made an even bigger success out of it. Over time, he became one of the leaders of the community, someone parents pointed out to their children as an example of what they would like them to grow up to be.

Major transformations are often like Joe's story. Some small event occurs that we would never have realized in advance was going to have a major impact on our lives. Some thought that had never occurred to us before keeps coming up over and over in our minds, gradually leading to a change in our personality. In Joe's case, the word *gentleman* must have triggered within him a new, possible model of himself, one that he wasn't aware of, yet one that pulled him in a new direction. Sometimes that change can't be seen for a very long time in our outer lives, which continue as if nothing had happened. Then one day, we can no longer stand the life we are living and nothing seems to make sense. Yet hidden away in the chaos that swallows up our life is the tiny kernel of change that eventually leads to a new personality emerging.

Joe's story is just a small example of how one's life can be taken apart, then put back together in an entirely new form. The girl's comment led to a bifurcation, a strikingly new direction in his life. A tiny change, his attempt to become a gentleman, through *feedback*, eventually permeated his whole life. Though it's only implicit in the story, it is likely that before he met the girl, Joe was already falling into *chaos*. Career criminals learn to do their time in prison with as little fuss as possible so they can return to their life of crime. In contrast, Joe fought so hard against the rules that he spent his time isolated from any human contact. Once out of prison he immediately returned to the type of overt crimes that would undoubtedly lead him back into a prison life he couldn't stand. The final person he became could never have been seen in his actions up to the point of meeting the girl, but somehow that transformation *emerged* out of the chaos. He was, as complexity theorists would say, living at the edge of chaos, with crime forming an attractor that was pulling him ineluctably toward a terrible outcome. But then a new attractor formed, quite literally by his "attraction" to this young woman. Undoubtedly it wasn't as straightforward as the story makes it sound. There must have been untold cycles where Joe had to take apart the way he had previously done things and put them back together in a new way that was consistent with the image of a gentleman. Throughout that process, changes he made within himself led to outer changes, which in turn led back to inner changes. As above, so below, through feedback. And the goal that Joe was seeking unconsciously, his philosopher's stone, turned out to be his own self-transformation.

If that could happen in Joe's life, if he could find his philosopher's stone, so too can all of us.

Indra's Net

Central to this book is the understanding that the opus is within us as much as it is without. As I mentioned in the introduction, Buddhist philosophy captures this relationship between the world and the psyche through the image of Indra's net: a vast necklace of shining jewels, all interconnected. It is told thus in the Avatamsaka Sutra:

> Far away in the heavenly abode of the great god Indra, there is a wonderful net which has been hung by some cunning artificer in such a manner that it stretches out infinitely in all directions. In accordance with the extravagant tastes of deities, the artificer has hung a single glittering jewel in each "eye" of the net, and since the net itself is infinite in dimension, the jewels are infinite in number. There hang the jewels, glittering like stars in the first

magnitude, a wonderful sight to behold. If we now arbitrarily select one of these jewels for inspection and look closely at it, we will discover that in its polished surface there are reflected *all* the other jewels in the net, infinite in number. Not only that, but each of the jewels reflected in this one jewel is also reflecting all the other jewels, so that there is an infinite reflecting process occurring.[38]

This notion has been a central metaphor both in the East and the West. In Buddhist philosophy, Indra's net is used as a symbol of how totally interconnected all reality is. I first encountered this idea not through the Buddhist metaphor but though an expression of it in an essay, "Pascal's Sphere," by the great Argentine writer Jorge Luis Borges. Borges began that essay by remarking that "perhaps universal history is the history of a few metaphors. I should like to sketch one chapter of that history." He proceeds to tell the story of the famous idea, which we have already encountered, that "God is an intelligible sphere whose center is everywhere and whose circumference is nowhere," as Alain de Lille put it. He ends the essay by saying, "perhaps universal history is the history of the diverse intonation of a few metaphors."[39] Somehow I always remember the last sentence incorrectly as "perhaps universal history is the history of the diverse intonation of a *single* metaphor." Perhaps I hear it that way because, for me, this sphere is the single metaphor that describes the most essential quality of reality, both outer and inner.

Borges' history begins with the Greek writer Xenophanes in the sixth century BC, who proposed that God was an eternal sphere. He follows the evolution of that image through Plato, then Parmenides and Empedocles. The idea first appeared in its entirety in the words of Alain de Lille, a twelfth-century theologian, and was included as part of the Hermetica (introduced in chapter 2 in our discussion of the Emerald Tablet). By the time of philosopher Giordano Bruno, in the late sixteenth century, the "universe" had replaced "God" in the metaphor; Bruno says, "We can state with certainty that the universe is all center, or that the center of the universe is everywhere and the circumference nowhere." Borges gets the title of his essay from Pascal's version, which is the same as de Lille's except that "nature" has replaced "God." But of more interest to Borges, he found in a critical edition of Pascal that he had originally intended to write "a *frightful* sphere, the center of which is everywhere, and the circumference nowhere [emphasis mine]."

Throughout this book, we have seen various approximations to this metaphor in both alchemy and chaos theory. For example, in the alchemy section of chapter 2, which explored the idea of "as above, so below," we traced the "diverse intonation" (to use Borges' phrase) of the idea that the *above* (the heavens or the spirit) and the *below* (the physical world or the world of our personal bodies) are inextricably united. In the chaos theory section of that chapter, we saw this idea appear in a seemingly very different expression in the model of fractals, which are self-similar at all levels.

The alchemical section of chapter 3, on feedback, provided us with the symbol of the uroboros, the snake that swallows its tail. This image symbolizes the idea that the end is already contained within the beginning. We saw that chaos theory emerged from the idea of feedback, where the end of each cycle in nature automatically becomes the starting point for the next cycle, much like the uroboros. And both can exist only in a universe where everything is connected to everything else, where everything reflects everything else.

Indra's net isn't as easy to see in the insights from chapter 4, on "take apart, put together," but it is there nonetheless, albeit in some disguise. We remarked there that the alchemical opus was frequently summarized as "dissolve and coagulate." Implicit in this phrase is the idea that each of the pieces that are taken apart is in some way a reflection of the whole. How else could they reassemble, without that underlying connection? And with Raymond Lull's primitive computers, we saw that (at least in Lull's mind) no matter how you turned the dials, you could find ultimate truth, because each dial pointed to an aspect of God. In a way, he was saying that God is an infinite sphere whose center is everywhere. In the chaos theory section, we again find a permutation of this central theme in the model of attractors, especially in the description of how the baker's transformation produces a strange attractor. To see the parallel, consider

146

the baker's kneaded dough as the whole universe. *Davies' magic* When you knead it, nothing is taken away or added, yet any particular point can end up at any other place in the loaf. They become interchangeable, each a reflection of the whole. And even with simpler attractors, no matter where you begin, you follow a path that ends up within the attractor. Thus, the center—the attractor—is everywhere.

As I remarked in chapter 5, on chaos and emergence, the alchemical image of sparks of light appearing in the darkness touched off my realization that alchemy and chaos theory might be presenting the same model, since chaos theory offers an almost identical image of new order forming. I offered a prosaic example of emergence of order: the transition that occurs as water comes to a boil. But I also discussed more complex physical versions, such as a slime mold cell's transition back and forth between being an individual or a cell in a group organism. But let's return to the alchemical image of emergence, since it comes so close to the symbol of Indra's net. At the transition point in the alchemical opus between the *nigredo* and *albedo* stages, alchemists reported that they saw scintillae of light appear in the darkness. Lights would appear and disappear, seemingly at random, perhaps the lights of new consciousness attempting to form into one united consciousness, like the diamonds sparkling in Indra's net.

It is my profound hope that this book has lit sparks of light in you, sparks that will come together into a single, ever-brighter light, one that can help transform your life as it has transformed the lives of so many other explorers of the inner world, whether they call themselves students of alchemy or students of chaos.

~The Philosopher's Stone~

Notes

Foreword

Epigraph. N. J. Girardot, *Myth and Meaning in Early Taoism* (Berkeley: University of California Press, 1983), 3.

Introduction

Epigraph. Julius Evola, *The Hermetic Tradition: Symbols and Teachings of the Royal Art*, trans. E. E. Rehmus (Rochester, VT: Inner Traditions International, 1971), 27.

1. From a letter from Atwood to C. C. Massey, quoted in the introduction to the 1920 edition of *A Suggestive Inquiry into the Hermetic Mystery* by Mary Anne Atwood (Belfast: William Tait, 1920), 30. The original edition (London: Trelawney Saunders, 1850) was published anonymously by the then Mary Anne South and withdrawn six weeks later by South and her father and intellectual companion, Thomas South, for fear that it revealed secrets that were intended to remain hidden.

2. E. A. Hitchcock, *Remarks on Alchemy and the Alchemists* (Boston: Crosby, Nichols and Co., 1857), iv.

3. Herbert Silberer, *Problems of Mysticism and Its Symbolism*, trans. Smith Ely Jellife (New York: Moffat, Yard and Co., 1917; New York: Samuel Weiser, Inc., 1970). Citations are to the Samuel Weiser edition.

4. Some of this information was drawn from *Wikipedia*, s.v. "Herbert Silberer," http://en.wikipedia.org/wiki/Herbert_Silberer (accessed September 1, 2007).

5. C. G. Jung, *Collected Works*, vol. 12, *Psychology and Alchemy*, 2nd ed., Bollingen Series 20 (Princeton, NJ: Princeton University Press, 1968), par. 332.

6. Mircea Eliade, *The Forge and the Crucible*, 2nd ed., trans. Stephen Corrin (Chicago: University of Chicago Press, 1978), 223.

7. Ibid., 224.

8. Ibid.

9. James Gleick, *Chaos: Making a New Science* (New York: Viking Penguin, 1987), 322.

10. Stephen H. Kellert, *In the Wake of Chaos* (Chicago and London: University of Chicago Press, 1993), xi.

11. Walter J. Freeman, *Societies of Brains: A Study in the Neuroscience of Love and Hate* (Hillsdale, NJ: Erlbaum, 1995), 18.

12. This idea was thought to have originated in the *Corpus Hermeticum* of the third century. It later found many variant expressions in authors as famous as Pascal and Emerson.

Chapter 1

Epigraph. <http://www.wisdomquotes.com/cat_history.html> (accessed October 1, 2008).

1. Richard Grossinger, *Alchemy: Pre-Egyptian Legacy, Millennial Promise* (Richmond, CA: North Atlantic Books, 1979), 177.

2. Eliade, *The Forge and the Crucible*, 169 (see intro., n. 6).

3. C. A. Burland, *The Art of the Alchemists* (New York: Macmillan, 1968), 7–8.

4. Much of this history came from *Wikipedia*, s.v. "Library of Alexandria," http://en.wikipedia.org/wiki/Library_of_Alexandria (accessed February 1, 2007).

5. Johannes Fabricius, *Alchemy: The Medieval Alchemists and Their Royal Art* (Copenhagen: Rosenkilde and Bagger, 1976), 7.

6. Isaac Newton, "The Commentary on the Emerald Tablet," in *The Alchemy Reader: From Hermes Trismegistus to Isaac Newton*, ed. Stanton J. Linden (Cambridge: Cambridge University Press, 2003), 247.

7. Both quotes from Eliade, *The Forge and the Crucible*, 232–33.

8. Walter J. Freeman, foreword to Robin Robertson and Allan Combs, eds., *Chaos Theory in Psychology and the Life Sciences* (Mahwah, NJ: Lawrence Erlbaum Associates, 1995), x.

9. Gleick, *Chaos*, 18 (see intro., n. 9).

10. Though Lorenz has deservedly captured the popular imagination as the discoverer of chaos theory, great ideas tend to be "in the air" at a given point. At virtually the same time that Lorenz was making his great discovery, Japanese mathematician Yoshisuke Ueda also discovered "strange attractors" (see chapter 4) and chaos (which he termed "randomly transitional phenomena"). Besides Lorenz and Ueda, many other major figures in science and mathematics contributed to the early development of chaos theory. For details on the history of these ideas, see Ralph Abraham and Yoshisuke Ueda, eds., *The Chaos Avant-Garde: Memories of the Early Days of Chaos Theory* (Singapore: World Scientific Co., 2000).

Chapter 2

Epigraph. Brian P. Coperhaver, trans., *Hermetica: The Greek Corpus Hermeticum and the Latin Asclepius* (Cambridge: Cambridge University Press, 1992), 36.

1. Jolande Jacobi, ed., *Paracelsus: Selected Writings*, Bollingen Series 28 (Princeton, NJ: Princeton University Press, 1951), 93.

2. Quoted in B. J. Dobbs, "Newton's Commentary on the Emerald Tablet of Hermes Trismegistus," in I. Merkel and A. G. Debus, eds., *Hermeticism and the Renaissance* (Washington, DC: Folger, 1988), 183–84. Text retreived from The Alchemy Web Site, "Emerald Tablet of Hermes," http://www.alchemywebsite.com/emerald.html (accessed March 1, 2007). Spelling regularized by the present author.

3. Much of this history is adapted from E. J. Holmyard, *Alchemy* (New York: Dover, 1990), 100.

4. Copenhaver, *Hermetica*, xlviii.

5. See Copenhaver, *Hermetica*, xiv, for this particular example, as well as for much of the scholarly information post-Holmyard.

6. *Wikipedia*, s.v. "Emerald Tablet," http://en.wikipedia.org/wiki/Emerald_Tablet (accessed March 1, 2007).

7. Marie-Louise von Franz, *Alchemy: An Introduction to the Symbolism and the Psychology* (Toronto: Inner City Books, 1980), 11.

8. Carolyn Dewald, ed., *Herodotus: The Histories*, trans. Robin Waterfield (Oxford: Oxford University Press, 1988), 144.

9. Diogenes Laertius, "The Life of Pythagoras," in Kenneth S. Guthrie, *The Pythagorean Sourcebook and Library* (Grand Rapids, MI: Phanes Press, 1987) 148.

10. Ibid.

11. See David Fideler's introduction to Guthrie, *The Pythagorean Sourcebook and Library*, particularly page 36.

12. Stephan A. Hoeller, "How to Understand Gnosticism," *Gnosis Magazine* 2 (Spring/Summer 1986): 4.

13. C. G. Jung, "Paracelsus the Physician," in *Collected Works*, vol. 15, *The Spirit in Man, Art, and Literature*, Bollingen Series 20 (Princeton, NJ: Princeton University Press, 1942), par. 2.

14. Ibid., par. 6.

15. Adapted from *Wikipedia*, s.v. "Paracelsus," http://en.wikipedia.org/wiki/Paracelsus (accessed March 28, 2007).

16. Jung, "Paracelsus the Physician," par. 16.

17. Jacobi, *Paracelsus*, 113.

18. Ibid., 92.

19. Ibid., 229.

20. Ibid., 227.

21. Jon Marshall, *Jung, Alchemy and History: A Critical Exposition of Jung's Theory of Alchemy*, Hermetic Research Series 12 (Glasgow, UK: Adam McLean, 2002), 12.

22. Jacobi, *Paracelsus*, 194.

23. Jung, "Paracelsus the Physician," par. 26.

24. All Paracelsus quotations in ibid., par. 42.

25. F. D. Abraham, *A Visual Introduction to Dynamical Systems Theory for Psychology* (Santa Cruz, CA: Aerial Press, 1992), chap. I, 1–3.

26. Jacobi, *Paracelsus*, 39.

27. Benoit Mandelbrot, "How Long is the Coast of Britain? Statistical Self-Similarity and Fractional Dimension," *Science* 156 (1967): 636–38.

28. Benoit Mandelbrot, *The Fractal Geometry of Nature* (New York: W. H. Freeman & Co., 1977), 29.

29. Benoit Mandelbrot, quoted in Ed Regis, *Who Got Einstein's Office?* (New York: Addison-Wesley Publishing Co., 1987), 89–90.

30. Isaac Asimov, *I, Asimov: A Memoir* (New York: Bantam, 1995). Quoted in Clifford A. Pickover, *A Passion for Mathematics* (Hoboken, NJ: John Wiley & Sons, 2005), 90.

31. $Z_{n+1} = Z_n + c$, where c is a complex number; that is, a number with both a real and an imaginary component.

32. Hoeller, "How to Understand Gnosticism," 4.

33. R. D. Laing, *Knots* (New York: Pantheon Books, 1970), 50.

34. Terry Marks-Tarlow, "The Fractal Geometry of Human Nature," in Robertson and Combs, *Chaos Theory*, 277 (see chap. 1, n. 8).

35. William Wordsworth, "The Rainbow," in *William Wordsworth: Selected Poems and Prefaces*, ed. Jack Stillinger (Boston: Houghton Mifflin Co., 1965).

Chapter 3

Epigraph. Steve Heims, *The Cybernetics Group* (Cambridge, MA: MIT Press, 1991), 271.

1. E. J. Holmyard, *Alchemy*, 52 (see chap. 2, n. 3).

2. Quoted in James Gleick, *Isaac Newton* (New York: Pantheon Books, 2003), 93.

3. *Pistis Sophia,* A Fourth Book, chap. 126, The Gnostic Archive, http://www.gnosis.org/library/psoph.htm (accessed May 9, 2007).

4. *Pistis Sophia,* A Fifth Book, chap. 136, The Gnostic Archive, http://www.gnosis.org/library/psoph.htm (accessed May 9, 2007).

5. Johann Conrad Barchusen, *Elementa chemiae* (Leiden, 1718).

6. C. G. Jung, *Collected Works*, vol. 14, *Mysterium Coniunctionis*, Bollingen Series 20 (Princeton, NJ: Princeton University Press, 1970), par. 513.

Notes

7. The Chinese traditionally date Lao Tzu and the *Tao Te Ching* to the sixth century BC, but historians believe the fourth century BC is more accurate.

8. Lao Tzu, *Tao Te Ching*, trans. Raymond B. Blakney (n.p.: n.p., 1955), chap. 42. Text retrieved from the web site of Mountain Man Graphics, http://www.mountainman.com.au/taotrans.html (accessed September 5, 2005).

9. Heinz von Foerster (1911–2002) was a cybernetics pioneer whose aphorisms were widely circulated but rarely committed to print.

10. Gleick, *Chaos*, 18 (see intro., n. 9).

11. Francisco J. Varela, *Principles of Biological Autonomy* (New York: North Holland, 1979), 166–67.

12. For information on the Macy conferences, I'm drawing largely on Heims, *The Cybernetics Group*.

13. Heims, *The Cybernetics Group*, 15.

14. Ibid.

15. Warren McCulloch and Walter Pitts, "A Logical Calculus of the Ideas Immanent in Nervous Activity," *Bulletin of Mathematical Biophysics* 5 (1943): 115–33. Reproduced in James A. Anderson and Edward Rosenfeld, *Neurocomputing: Foundations of Research* (Cambridge, MA: MIT Press, 1988), 15–28.

16. Heims, *The Cybernetics Group*, 251.

17. See Gregory Bateson, *Steps to an Ecology of Mind* (New York: Ballantine Books, 1972) and *Mind and Nature: A Necessary Unity* (New York: E. Dutton, 1979).

18. Heims, *The Cybernetics Group*, 24. See Gregory Bateson, *Naven*, 6th ed. (Stanford: Stanford University Press, 1958) for a full description of this culture.

19. Heims, *The Cybernetics Group*, 24. Also see Norbert Wiener's related questions in his book *The Human Use of Human Beings: Cybernetics and Society*, rev. ed. (1950; New York: De Capo Press, 1954).

20. Mary Catherine Bateson, *Our Own Metaphor* (New York: Alfred A. Knopf, 1972), 16.

21. Ibid., 66–67.

22. Ibid.

23. Edward F. Edinger, *Anatomy of the Psyche: Alchemical Symbolism in Psychotherapy* (La Salle, IL: Open Court, 1985), 143.

24. Kate Marcus, "On Initial Dreams" (paper presented to the Analytical Psychology Club of Los Angeles, March, 1954), 8.

Chapter 4

Epigraph. Coperhaver, *Hermetica*, 28 (see chap. 2, epigraph).

1. Eliade, *The Forge and the Crucible*, 153 (see intro., n. 6).

2. Bonus of Ferrara, *The New Pearl of Great Price* (1546; London: Vincent Stuart, 1963), 365. Quoted in Edinger, *Anatomy of the Psyche*, 47 (see chap. 3, n. 23).

3. Artephius, *The Secret Book*, The Alchemy Web Site, http://www.levity.com/alchemy/artephiu.html, par. 40 (accessed July 13, 2007). Also see Edinger, *Anatomy of the Psyche*, 48.

4. C. G. Jung, "The Psychology of the Transference," *Collected Works*, vol. 16, *The Practice of Psychotherapy: Essays on the Psychology of the Transference and Other Subjects* (New York: Pantheon Books, Bollingen Foundation, 1954), 163–321.

5. William McGuire and R. F. C. Hull, eds., "Eliade's Interview for *Combat*," in *C. G. Jung Speaking*, Bollingen Series 97 (Princeton, NJ: Princeton University Press, 1977), 227.

6. Commentary attributed to Isaac Newton, "Emerald Tablet of Hermes," section "Commentaries," subsection "General," The Internet Sacred Text Archive, http://www.sacred-texts.com/alc/emerald.htm (accessed August 7, 2007).

7. "Summary of the Rosary of Arnold de Villa Nova," The Alchemy Web Site, http://www.alchemywebsite.com/arnoldus.html (accessed July 13, 2007).

8. See Charles Mackay, *Extraordinary Popular Delusions and the Madness of Crowds* (New York: Noonday Press, 1932), 112. Reprint of *Memoirs of Extraordinary Popular Delusions* (London: Richard Bentley, 1841).

9. Frances Yates, *The Occult Philosophy in the Elizabethan Age* (London and New York: Routledge & Kegan Paul, 1979), 12–13.

10. Étienne Gilson, quoted in Anne Fremantel, ed., *The Age of Belief: The Medieval Philosophers* (New York: Mentor Books, Houghton Mifflin, 1954), xii.

11. Edna E. Kramer, *The Nature and Growth of Modern Mathematics* (Princeton, NJ: Princeton University Press, 1970), 100.

12. W. L. Reese, *Dictionary of Philosophy and Religion* (New Jersey: Humanities Press and Sussex: Harvester Press, 1980), 319.

13. See Ibid., 319.

14. *Encyclopedia Americana*, international ed., s.v. "Lully, Raymond."

15. Frances Yates, *The Art of Memory* (Chicago: University of Chicago Press, 1966), 176.

16. John Briggs and F. David Peat, *Turbulent Mirror: An Illustrated Guide to Chaos Theory and the Science of Wholeness* (New York: Harper & Row, 1989), 110.

17. In my description of the logistics map in terms of the growth of the rabbit population, I have drawn on Briggs and Peat, *Turbulent Mirror*, ch. 3.

18. This is a somewhat simplified version of the equation developed by a Belgian mathematician, Pierre François Verhulst, in 1845. It's often called the *Verhulst Equation*.

19. The term *strange attractor* was coined by French–Belgian mathematical physicist David Ruelle in a paper coauthored with the Dutch physicist Floris Takens: D. Ruelle and F. Takens, "On the Nature of Turbulence," *Communications in Mathematical Physics* 20 (1971): 167–92 and 23 (1971): 343–44.

20. Bonus of Ferrara, *The New Pearl of Great Price*, 365.

21. I've given a brief account of this before in my book *Your Shadow* (Virginia Beach, VA: A.R.E. Press, 1997).

Chapter 5

Epigraph. Jack Cohen and Ian Stewart, *The Collapse of Chaos* (New York: Penguin Books, 1994), 232.

1. McGuire and Hull, eds., "Eliade's Interview for *Combat*," 229 (see chap. 4, n. 5).

2. All quotes in this discussion from Titus Burckhardt, *Alchemy* (Baltimore: Penguin Books, 1971), 182.

3. See in general Jung, *Collected Works*, vol. 14, *Mysterium Coniunctionis* (see chap. 3, n. 6).

4. Evola, *The Hermetic Tradition*, 31 (see intro., epigraph).

5. Fabricius, *Alchemy*, 98 (see chap. 1, n. 5). Text translated from the Latin of Raymond Lull's *Ultimum testamentum, Artis aurif., III,* page 1. Note that many such attributions to Lull may be spurious.

6. For an analysis of the act of distinction as presented in logician G. Spencer-Brown's *Laws of Form*, see Robin Robertson, "The Evolution of Jung's Archetypal Reality," *Psychological Perspectives* 41, no. 1 (2000): 66–80.

7. C. G. Jung, "*VII Sermones ad Mortuos*," trans. Stephan A. Hoeller, in Stephan A. Hoeller, *The Gnostic Jung and the Seven Sermons to the Dead* (Wheaton, IL: Quest Books, Theosophical Publishing House, 1982), 44. For a different translation by Richard and Clara Winston, see C. G. Jung, *Memories, Dreams, Reflections*, rev. ed. (New York: Pantheon Books, 1973), appendix V, "*Septum Sermones ad Mortuos*."

8. Michael Maier, *Atalanta fugiens*, trans. Jocelyn Godwin (1618; Grand Rapids, MI: Phanes Press, 1989), 111.

9. Evola, *The Hermetic Tradition*, 31 (see intro., epigraph).

10. Fabricius, *Alchemy*, 98.

11. McGuire and Hull, eds., "Eliade's Interview for *Combat*," 228 (see chap. 4, n.5).

12. Morienus, "The Book of Morienus," Rex Research web site, http://www.rexresearch.com/alchemy3/morienus.htm (accessed October 29, 2007). Sixteenth-century alchemical text, translated and edited by Lee Stavenhagen; published as *A Testament of Alchemy* (Hanover, NH: University Press of New England, 1974).

13. See in general Edinger, *Anatomy of the Psyche* (see chap. 3, n. 23).

14. Eliade, *The Forge and the Crucible*, 223 (see intro., n. 6).

15. All quotes from C. G. Jung, *Collected Works*, vol. 8, *The Structure and Dynamics of the Psyche*, 2nd ed., Bollingen Series 20 (Princeton, NJ: Princeton University Press, 1969), par. 388.

Notes

16. Mircea Eliade, *The Two and the One* (New York, Harper & Row, 1965), 43–45. Excerpted in Mircea Eliade, *Myths, Rites, Symbols: A Mircea Eliade Reader*, vol. 2, eds. William G. Doty and Wendell C. Beane (New York and San Francisco: Harper & Row, 1976), 333–34.

17. *Aurora consurgens: A Document Attributed to Thomas Aquinas on the Problem of Opposites in Alchemy*, ed. and commentator Marie-Louise von Franz; trans. R. F. C. Hull and A. S. B. Glover, Bollingen Series 77 (New York: Pantheon Books, 1966), 265.

18. Maier, *Atalanta fugiens*. 111.

19. Ibid., 131.

20. Ibid., 171.

21. Morienus, *Book of Morienus*.

22. Briggs and Peat, *Turbulent Mirror*, 75 (see chap. 4, n. 16).

23. Wallace Stevens, "The Idea of Order at Key West," in Manard Mack et al., eds., *Modern Poetry*, Vol. VII, 2nd ed. (Englewood Cliffs, NJ: Prentice-Hall, 1961), 292.

24. Bertrand Russell, *The Autobiography of Bertrand Russell,* vol. 1, *1872–1914* (Boston: Little, Brown and Co., 1967), 218.

25. For details on Russell's project and Godel's proof, see Robin Robertson, *Jungian Archetypes: Jung, Gödel, and the History of Archetypes* (York Beach, ME: Nicolas-Hays, Inc., 1995).

26. Kellert, *In the Wake of Chaos*, 49 (see intro., n. 10).

27. David Ruelle, *Chance and Chaos* (Princeton: Princeton University Press, 1991), 75. David Ruelle is one of the pioneers of chaos theory.

28. Marc Jeannerod, *The Brain Machine: The Development of Neurophysiological Thought* (Cambridge, MA: Harvard University Press, 1985), 2.

29. John Stuart Mill, *Logic* (London: Harris and Co., 1843). Quoted in Edwin G. Boring, *A History of Experimental Psychology*, 2nd ed. (New York: Appleton-Century-Crofts, Inc., 1950), 230. Mill's emphasis in all cases.

30. G. H. Lewes, *Problems of Life and Mind*, vol. 2 (London: Kegan Paul, Trench, Tubner, 1875), 368–69. Quoted in Jeffrey Goldstein, "Emergence as a Construct: History and Issues," *Emergence: Complexity and Organization* 1, no. 1 (1999): 53.

31. Ibid., Goldstein, "Emergence as a Construct: History and Issues," 49.

32. H. Ross Ashby, "Principles of the Self-Organizing System," in H. Von Foerster and G. W. Zopf, Jr., eds., *Principles of Self-Organization: Transactions of the University of Illinois Symposium* (London: Pergamon Press, 1962), 255–78. Reprinted in Kurt A. Richardson and Jeffrey A. Goldstein, eds., *Classic Complexity: From the Abstract to the Concrete* (Mansfield, MA: ISCE Publishing, 2007), 111–36.

33. Warren Weaver, "Science and Complexity," reprinted in Richardson and Goldstein, *Classic Complexity*, 154.

34. Ibid., 153.

35. Both quotes from ibid., 156.

36. F. David Peat, *The Philosopher's Stone: Chaos, Synchronicity, and the Hidden Order of the World* (New York: Bantam Books, 1991), 76–77.

Chapter 6

Epigraph. Heinrich Cornelius Agrippa, *De occulta philosophia*, 3:36. Quoted in Evola, *The Hermetic Tradition*, 25 (see intro., epigraph). Agrippa was an occult writer of the sixteenth century.

1. Eliade, *The Forge and the Crucible*, 165 (see intro., n. 6).

2. Ibid., 151–52.

3. Both quotes in ibid., 167.

4. Unknown author, attributed to Nicolas Flamel, *Nicolas Flamel and the Philosopher's Stone* (Whitefish, MT: Kessinger Publishing, 2005), 15.

5. Ibid., 16.

6. Both quotes from ibid., 47–48.

7. Information on books mentioning Flamel from *Wikipedia*, s.v. "Nicholas Flamel," http://en.wikipedia.org/wiki/Nicolas_Flamel, and *Wikipedia*, s.v. "List of Harry Potter characters," http://en.wikipedia.org/wiki/Historical_characters_in_Harry_Potter#Nicolas_Flamel (both accessed September 8, 2007).

8. Linden, ed., *The Alchemy Reader*, 123 (see chap. 1, n. 6).

9. *Nicolas Flamel and the Philosopher's Stone*, 7.

10. Ibid. A similar quote is in E. J. Holmyard, *Alchemy*, 240–41 (see chap. 2, n. 3).

Notes

11. Ibid., 8.

12. Ibid., 12, 14.

13. Patrick J. Smith, *The Book of the Hierographical Figures of Nicolas Flamel*, rev. ed. (Sequim, WA: Holmes Publishing Group, Alchemical Press, 2005), 46.

14. Linden, *The Alchemy Reader*, 123.

15. Grossinger, *Alchemy*, 248 (see chap. 1, n. 1).

16. Hitchcock, *Remarks on Alchemy*, 229 (see intro., n. 2).

17. Silberer, *Problems of Mysticism*, 342 (see intro., n. 3).

18. Ibid., 415.

19. Ibid., 342.

20. Ibid., 344.

21. Hitchcock, *Remarks on Alchemy*, 132.

22. <http://www.famousquotes.com/search.php?cat=1&search=Epitaphs> (accessed October 1, 2008).

23. Evola, *The Hermetic Tradition*, 14.

24. Paulo Coelho, *The Alchemist: A Fable about Following Your Dream*, trans. Alan R. Clarke (New York: HarperFlamingo, 1998), 138.

25. Quoted in Gleick, *Isaac Newton*, 93 (see chap. 3, n. 2).

26. Quoted in George Gamow, *The Great Physicists from Galileo to Einstein* (New York: Dover, 1988), 174.

27. Eliade, *The Forge and the Crucible*, 233.

28. Gleick, *Isaac Newton*, 100.

29. E. T. Bell, *Men of Mathematics* (1937; New York: Simon & Schuster, 1965), 172.

30. All quotes from Bell, *Men of Mathematics*, 181.

31. Ibid., 153.

32. Eliade, *The Forge and the Crucible*, 174.

33. Abraham, *A Visual Introduction* (see chap. 2, n. 25).

34. Freeman, *Societies of Brains*, 2 (see intro., n. 11).

35. Varela, *Principles of Biological Autonomy*, 13 (see chap. 3, n. 11).

36. Francisco J. Varela, "Intimate Distances: Fragments for a Phenomenology of Organ Transplantation," *Journal of Consciousness Studies* 8, nos. 5–7 (2001): 263.

37. Silberer, *Problems of Mysticism*, 336.

38. Francis Harold Cook, *Hua-Yen Buddhism: The Jewel Net of Indra* (University Park: Pennsylvania State University Press, 1977).

39. All quotes from Jorge Luis Borges, "Pascal's Sphere," *Other Inquisitions 1937–1952* (New York: Washington Square Press, 1965), 5–8.

Bibliography

Abraham, F. D. *A Visual Introduction to Dynamical Systems Theory for Psychology*. Santa Cruz, CA: Aerial Press, n.d.

Abraham, Ralph and Yoshisuke, Ueda, eds. *The Chaos Avante-Garde: Memories of the Early Days of Chaos Theory*. Singapore: World Scientific Co., 2000.

Agrippa, Heinrich Cornelius. *De occulta philosophia*. Quoted in Julius Evola, *The Hermetic Tradition: Symbols and Teachings of the Royal Art*, translated by E. E. Rehmus. Rochester, VT: Inner Traditions International, 1971.

Artephius. *The Secret Book*. The Alchemy Web Site, http://www.levity.com/alchemy/artephiu.html (accessed July 13, 2007).

Ashby, H. Ross. "Principles of the Self-Organizing System." In H. Von Foerster and G. W. Zopf, Jr., eds. *Principles of Self-Organization: Transactions of the University of Illinois Symposium*. London: Pergamon Press, 1962, 255–78. Reprinted in Kurt A. Richardson and Jeffrey A. Goldstein, eds. *Classic Complexity: From the Abstract to the Concrete*. Mansfield, MA: ISCE Publishing, 2007.

Atwood, Mary Anne. *A Suggestive Inquiry into the Hermetic Mystery*. Revised ed. Belfast: William Tait, 1920.

Barchusen, Johann Conrad. *Elementa chemiae*. Leiden, 1718.

Bateson, Gregory. *Mind and Nature: A Necessary Unity*. New York: E. Dutton, 1979.

———. *Steps to an Ecology of Mind*. New York: Ballantine Books, 1972.

Bateson, Mary Catherine. *Our Own Metaphor*. New York: Alfred A. Knopf, 1972.

Bell, E. T. *Men of Mathematics*. New York: Simon & Schuster, 1965.

Borges, Jorge Luis. "Pascal's Sphere." In *Other Inquisitions 1937–1952*. New York: Washington Square Press, 1965.

Bibliography

Briggs, John and F. David Peat. *Turbulent Mirror: An Illustrated Guide to Chaos Theory and the Science of Wholeness*. New York: Harper & Row, 1989.

Burckhardt, Titus. *Alchemy*. Baltimore: Penguin Books, 1971.

Burland, C. A. *The Art of the Alchemists*. New York: Macmillan, 1968.

Coelho, Paulo. *The Alchemist: A Fable about Following Your Dream*. Translated by Alan R. Clarke. New York: HarperFlamingo, 1998.

Cohen, Jack and Ian Stewart. *The Collapse of Chaos*. New York: Penguin Books, 1994.

Cook, Francis Harold. *Hua-Yen Buddhism: The Jewel Net of Indra*. University Park, PA: Pennsylvania State University Press, 1977.

Coperhaver, Brian P., trans. *Hermetica*. Cambridge: Cambridge University Press, 1992.

de Villa Nova, Arnold. "Summary of the Rosary of Arnold de Villa Nova." The Alchemy Web Site, http://www.alchemywebsite.com/arnoldus.html (accessed July 13, 2007).

Dewald, Carolyn, ed. *Herodotus: The Histories*. Translated by Robin Waterfield. Oxford: Oxford University Press, 1988.

Diogenes Laertius. "The Life of Pythagoras." In Kenneth S. Guthrie, *The Pythagorean Sourcebook and Library*. Grand Rapids, MI: Phanes Press, 1987.

Dobbs, B. J. "Newton's Commentary on the Emerald Tablet of Hermes Trismegistus." In I. Merkel and A. G. Debus, eds., *Hermeticism and the Renaissance*, 183–84. Washington: Folger, 1988.

Edinger, Edward F. *Anatomy of the Psyche: Alchemical Symbolism in Psychotherapy*. La Salle, IL: Open Court, 1985.

Eliade, Mircea. *The Forge and the Crucible*. 2nd ed. Translated by Stephen Corrin. Chicago: University of Chicago Press, 1978.

———. *The Two and the One*. New York: Harper & Row, 1965, 43–45. Excerpted in Mircea Eliade, *Myths, Rites, Symbols: A Mircea Eliade Reader*, vol. 2, edited by William G. Doty and Wendell C. Beane. New York and San Francisco: Harper & Row, 1976.

Encyclopedia Americana, international ed., s.v. "Lully, Raymond."

Bibliography

Evola, Julius, *The Hermetic Tradition: Symbols and Teachings of the Royal Art.* Translated by E. E. Rehmus. Rochester, VT: Inner Traditions International, 1971.

Fabricius, Johannes. *Alchemy: The Medieval Alchemists and Their Royal Art.* Copenhagen: Rosenkilde and Bagger, 1976.

Flamel, Nicolas (attributed to). *Nicolas Flamel and the Philosopher's Stone.* Whitefish, MT: Kessinger Publishing, 2005.

Freeman, Walter J. "Foreword." In Robin Robertson and Allan Combs, eds., *Chaos Theory in Psychology and the Life Sciences.* Mahwah, NJ: Lawrence Erlbaum Associates, 1995.

———. *Societies of Brains: A Study in the Neuroscience of Love and Hate.* Hillsdale, NJ: Erlbaum, 1995.

Gamow, George. *The Great Physicists from Galileo to Einstein.* New York: Dover, 1988.

Gilson, Étienne. Quoted in Anne Fremantel, ed., *The Age of Belief: The Medieval Philosophers.* New York: Mentor Books, Houghton Mifflin, 1954.

Girardot, N. J. *Myth and Meaning in Early Taoism.* Berkeley, CA: University of California Press, 1983.

Gleick, James. *Chaos: Making a New Science.* New York: Viking Penguin, 1987.

———. *Isaac Newton.* New York: Pantheon Books, 2003.

Grossinger, Richard. *Alchemy: Pre-Egyptian Legacy, Millennial Promise.* Richmond, CA: North Atlantic Books, 1979), 177.

Heims, Steve. *The Cybernetics Group.* Cambridge, MA: MIT Press, 1991.

Hitchcock, E. A. *Remarks on Alchemy and the Alchemists.* Boston: Crosby, Nichols, and Co., 1857.

Hoeller, Stephan A. "How to Understand Gnosticism," *Gnosis Magazine* 2. Spring/Summer 1986.

Jacobi, Jolande, ed. *Paracelsus: Selected Writings.* Bollingen Series 28. Princeton, NJ: Princeton University Press, 1951.

Jeannerod, Marc. *The Brain Machine: The Development of Neurophysiological Thought.* Cambridge, MA: Harvard University Press, 1985.

Bibliography

Jung, C. G. "Paracelsus." In *Collected Works*, vol. 15, *The Spirit in Man, Art, and Literature*. Bollingen Series 20. Princeton: Princeton University Press, 1942.

———. "The Psychology of the Transference." In *Collected Works*, vol. 16, *The Practice of Psychotherapy: Essays on the Psychology of the Transference and Other Subjects*. New York: Pantheon Books, Bollingen Foundation, 1954.

———. "*VII Sermones ad Mortuos*." Translated by Stephan A. Hoeller in Stephan A. Hoeller, *The Gnostic Jung and the Seven Sermons to the Dead*. Wheaton, IL: Quest Books, Theosophical Publishing House, 1982.

———. *Collected Works of C. G. Jung*. Vol. 12, *Psychology and Alchemy*. 2nd ed. Bollingen Series 20. Princeton: Princeton University Press, 1968.

———. *Collected Works*. Vol. 14, *Mysterium Coniunctionis*. Edited by G. Adler and R. F. Hull. Bollingen Series 20. Princeton,: Princeton University Press, 1963.

———. *Memories, Dreams, Reflections*. Revised ed. New York: Pantheon Books, 1973. Appendix V, "*Septum Sermones ad Mortuos*."

———. "Paracelsus the Physician." In *Collected Works*, vol. 15, *The Spirit in Man, Art, and Literature*. Bollingen Series 20. Princeton: Princeton University Press, 1942.

Kellert, Stephen H. *In the Wake of Chaos*. Chicago and London: University of Chicago Press, 1993.

Kramer, Edna E. *The Nature and Growth of Modern Mathematics*. Princeton: Princeton University Press, 1970.

Laing, R. D. *Knots*. New York: Pantheon Books, 1970.

Lao Tzu. *Tao Tè Ching*. Translated by Raymond B. Blakney. N.p.: n.p. 1955.

Lewes, G. H. *Problems of Life and Mind*. Vol. 2. London: Kegan Paul, Trench, Tubner, 368–69. Quoted in Jeffrey Goldstein, "Emergence as a Construct: History and Issues," *Emergence: Complexity and Organization* 1, no. 1 (1999): 49–72.

Linden, Stanton J. *The Alchemy Reader*. Cambridge: Cambridge University Press, 2003.

Mackay, Charles. *Extraordinary Popular Delusions and the Madness of Crowds*. New York: Noonday Press, 1932, 112. Reprint of *Memoirs of Extraordinary Popular Delusions*. London: Richard Bentley, 1841.

Maier, Michael. *Atalanta Fugiens.* Translated by Jocelyn Godwin. Grand Rapids, MI: Phanes Press, 1989. Originally published in 1618.

Mandelbrot, Benoit. "How Long Is the Coast of Britain? Statistical Self-Similarity and Fractional Dimension," *Science* 156, no. 3775 (May 5, 1967): 636–38.

Marcus, Kate. "On Initial Dreams." Paper presented to the Analytical Psychology Club of Los Angeles, March 1954.

Marks-Tarlow, Terry. "The Fractal Geometry of Human Nature." In Robin Robertson and Allan Combs, eds., *Chaos Theory in Psychology and the Life Sciences*. Mahweh, NJ: Lawrence Erlbaum, 1995.

Marshall, Jon. *Jung, Alchemy and History: A Critical Exposition of Jung's Theory of Alchemy*. Hermetic Research Series 12. Glasgow, UK: Adam McLean, 2002.

McCulloch, Warren and Walter Pitts. "A Logical Calculus of the Ideas Immanent in Nervous Activity." *Bulletin of Mathematical Biophysics* 5 (1943): 115–33. Reproduced in James A. Anderson and Edward Rosenfeld, *Neurocomputing: Foundations of Research*. Cambridge, MA: MIT Press, 1988.

McGuire, William and R. F. C. Hull, eds. "Eliade's Interview for *Combat*." In *C. G. Jung Speaking*, Bollingen Series 97. Princeton: Princeton University Press, 1977.

Mill, John Stuart. *Logic*. London: Harris and Co., 1843. Quoted in Edwin G. Boring, *A History of Experimental Psychology*, 2nd ed. New York: Appleton-Century-Crofts, Inc., 1950.

Morienus. "The Book of Morienus." Rex Research web site, http://www.rexresearch.com/alchemy3/morienus.htm (accessed October 29, 2007).

Newton, Isaac. Commentary attributed to Isaac Newton in "Emerald Tablet of Hermes," section "Commentaries," subsection "General." The Internet Sacred Text Archive, http://www.sacred-texts.com/alc/emerald.htm (accessed August 7, 2007).

———. "The Commentary on the Emerald Tablet." In Stanton J. Linden, ed., *The Alchemy Reader: From Hermes Trismegistus to Isaac Newton*. Cambridge: Cambridge University Press, 2003.

Peat, F. David. *The Philosopher's Stone: Chaos, Synchronicity, and the Hidden Order of the World*. New York: Bantam Books, 1991.

Bibliography

Pickover, Clifford A. *A Passion for Mathematics*. Hoboken, NJ: John Wiley & Sons, 2005.

Pistis Sophia. A Fifth Book, chap. 136. The Gnostic Archive, http://www. gnosis.org/library/psoph.htm (accessed May 9, 2007).

Pistis Sophia. A Fourth Book, chap. 126. The Gnostic Archive, http:// www.gnosis.org/library/psoph.htm (accessed May 9, 2007).

Reese, W. L. *Dictionary of Philosophy and Religion*. New Jersey: Humanities Press and Sussex: Harvester Press, 1980.

Regis, Ed. *Who Got Einstein's Office?* New York: Addison-Wesley Publishing Co., 1987.

Robertson, Robin. *Jungian Archetypes: Jung, Gödel and the History of Archetypes.* York Beach, ME: Nicolas-Hays, Inc., 1995.

———. *Your Shadow.* Virginia Beach, VA: A.R.E. Press, 1997.

Ruelle, D. and F. Takens. "On the Nature of Turbulence." *Communications in Mathematical Physics* 20 (1971): 167–92. See also vol. 23, 1971.

Ruelle, David. *Chance and Chaos*. Princeton: Princeton University Press, 1991.

Russell, Bertrand. *The Autobiography of Bertrand Russell, vol. 1, 1872–1914.* Boston: Little, Brown and Co., 1967.

Silberer, Herbert, *Problems of Mysticism and Its Symbolism.* Translated by Smith Ely Jellife. New York: Moffat, Yard and Co., 1917; New York: Samuel Weiser, Inc., 1970.

Smith, Patrick J. *The Book of the Hierographical Figures of Nicolas Flamel.* Revised ed. Sequim, WA: Holmes Publishing Group, Alchemical Press, 2005.

Stevens, Wallace. "The Idea of Order at Key West." In Manard Mack et al., eds., *Modern Poetry*, vol. 7, 2nd ed. Englewood Cliffs, NJ: Prentice-Hall, 1961.

Varela, Francisco J. "Intimate Distances: Fragments for a Phenomenology of Organ Transplantation." *Journal of Consciousness Studies* 8, nos. 5–7 (2001).

———. *Principles of Biological Autonomy*. New York: North Holland, 1979.

von Franz, Marie-Louise, ed. *Aurora consurgens: A Document Attributed to Thomas Aquinas on the Problem of Opposites in Alchemy.* Translated by

Bibliography

R. F. C. Hull and A. S. B. Glover. Bollingen Series 77. New York: Pantheon Books, 1966.

von Franz, Marie-Louise. *Alchemy: An Introduction to the Symbolism and the Psychology.* Toronto: Inner City Books, 1980.

Warren Weaver, "Science and Complexity." Reprinted in Kurt A. Richardson and Jeffrey A. Goldstein, eds., *Classic Complexity: From the Abstract to the Concrete.* Mansfield, MA: ISCE Publishing, 2007.

Wikipedia, s.v. "Emerald Tablet," http://en.wikipedia.org/wiki/Emerald_Tablet (accessed March 1, 2007).

———. "Herbert Silberer," http://en.wikipedia.org/wiki/Herbert_Silberer (accessed September 1, 2007).

———. "Library of Alexandria," http://en.wikipedia.org/wiki/Library_of_Alexandria (accessed February 1, 2007).

———. "Paracelsus," http://en.wikipedia.org/wiki/Paracelsus (accessed March 28, 2007).

Wordsworth, William. "The Rainbow." In Jack Stillinger, ed., *William Wordsworth: Selected Poems and Prefaces.* Boston: Houghton Mifflin Company, 1965.

Yates, Frances. *The Art of Memory.* Chicago: University of Chicago Press, 1966.

———. *The Occult Philosophy in the Elizabethan Age.* London & New York: Routledge & Kegan Paul, 1979.

Illustration Credits

1.1 Joannes Jacobus Mangetus, ed., *Bibliotheca chemica curiosa*, vol. I, (Geneva, 1702), vii–a.

2.1 Balanced Approaches web site, http://balancedapproaches.com/yinYang.gif (accessed April 23, 2007).

2.2 *Wikipedia*, image "KochFlake," http://en.wikipedia.org/wiki/Koch_snowflake (accessed April 23, 2007).

2.3 *Wikipedia*, image "Von_Koch_curve," http://en.wikipedia.org/wiki/Image:
Von_Koch_curve.gif (accessed April 23, 2007).

2.4 *Wikipedia*, image "Sierpinski_triangle," http://en.wikipedia.org/wiki/Image:Sierpinski_Triangle.svg (accessed April 23, 2007).

2.5 *Wikipedia*, image "Sierpinski_carpet_6," http://en.wikipedia.org/wiki/Image:Sierpinski_carpet_6.png (accessed April 23, 2007).

2.6 *Wikipedia*, image "Menger_sponge," http://en.wikipedia.org/wiki/Image:
Menger_sponge.png (accessed April 23, 2007).

2.7 Generated using Xaos freeware program, http://xaos.sourceforge.net/english.php.

3.1 From *Codex Marcianus*, 11th century. Reproduced in C. G. Jung, *Collected Works*, vol. 12, *Psychology and Alchemy*, 2nd ed. Bollingen Series 20 (Princeton, NJ: Princeton University Press, 1968), 293.

3.2 "Ouroborous," Crystalinks, image file at http://www.crystalinks.com/ouroborosaztec.jpg; image linked from http://www.crystalinks.com/ouroboros.html (accessed August 9, 2008).

3.3 Johann Conrad Barchusen, *Elementa chemiae* (Leiden, 1718).

3.4 Johann Daniel Mylius, *Philosophia reformata* (Frankfort, 1622).

Illustration Credits

3.5 Hieronymus Reusner, *Pandora* (Basel, 1582).

3.6 *Wikipedia*, s.v. "Klein bottle," http://en.wikipedia.org/wiki/Image: Klein_bottle.svg (accessed October 23, 2008).

3.7 Hieronymus Reusner, *Pandora* (Basel, 1582).

3.8 "Free mandala," The Green Centre, London, England, http://www. thegreencentre.com/mandala.php (accessed September 2, 2008).

4.1 *Rosarium Philosorum* (Frankfort, 1550).

4.2 *Rosarium Philosorum* (Frankfort, 1550).

4.3 *Rosarium Philosorum* (Frankfort, 1550).

4.4 Raymond Lull, *Ars brevis* (Strasburg, 1617), in Frances A. Yates, *The Art of Memory* (Chicago: University of Chicago Press, 1966), 182.

4.5 *Wikipedia*, image "LogisticMap BifurcationDiagram," http:// en.wikipedia.org/wiki/Image:LogisticMap_BifurcationDiagram.png (accessed September 2, 2008).

4.6 R. Lewis, Fordham University, http://www.fordham.edu/lewis/ fferm/torus.png (accessed September 2, 2008).

4.7 Arnold Keyserling and R.C.L., "Number," Chap. 2 in *Chance and Choice: A Compendium of Ancient and Modern Wisdom Revealing the Meaning and Significance of the Myth of Science*, http://www.chancean-dchoice.com/ChanceandChoice/torus.jpg (accessed September 2, 2008).

4.8 "The Lorenz Attractor" (animation) at http://turnex.dk/chaos/ lorenz.html; static image file at http://turnex.dk/chaos/lorenz_ attractor02.gif (accessed September 2, 2008).

5.1 Michael Maier, *Atalanta fugiens* (Frankfort, 1617), emblema L.

5.2 Michael Maier, *Atalanta fugiens* (Frankfort, 1617), emblema III.

5.3 Michael Maier, *Atalanta fugiens* (Frankfort, 1617), emblema XIII.

5.4 Michael Maier, *Atalanta fugiens* (Frankfort, 1617), emblema XXXIII.

5.5 Andrew Rooke, "Roadmaps for Spiritual Paths," http://www. theosophy-nw.org/theosnw/world/asia/as-rook2.htm; image file at http://www.theosophy-nw.org/theosnw/world/asia/s6amar-oh4.jpg (accessed September 2, 2008).

5.6 Andrew Rooke, "Roadmaps for Spiritual Paths," http://www. theosophy-nw.org/theosnw/world/asia/as-rook2.htm; image file at

Illustration Credits

http://www.theosophy-nw.org/theosnw/world/asia/s6amar-oh10.jpg (accessed September 2, 2008).

5.7 See figure 4.5.

6.1 *Wikipedia*, image "Flamel-figures," http://commons.wikimedia.org/wiki/Image:Flamel-figures.png (accessed September 2, 2008).

Index

175

Index

Index

Index

Index

Index

of alchemist, 7, 51–52, 127–28, 129
"as above, so below" and, 39–42
autopoiesis in, 141–42
being cut into pieces in, 85–87
dynamic method of, 87–88
emergence and, 113–17
feedback and, 62–65
sensitive dependence, 3–4, 18, 103
sensory stimuli, 137
separatio (separating), 44, 68, 70–71, 72
Set, 69
shadow stage, 94
Sierpinski, Waclaw
geometric forms of, 35
Silberer, Herbert, 2, 129–30
slime mold, 111–12
Smith, Patrick J., 125
Societies of Brains (Freeman), 137
Sol (sun), 68, 69, 70, 71
solutio (dissolving), 6, 44, 63, 67–73,
85, 98–99
soul, 93, 94, 128, 146
in Greek thought, 24–27
square, 53–54, 74
"square the circle," 53–54
Stevens, Wallace, 103
Stewart, Ian, 89
stimulus-response chains, 56, 136
strange attractors, 83–85, 109
sublimatio (sublimating), 5, 44, 63, 68,
70–71
sulphur, 68–69, 72, 120
sun, 25, 68, 70, 71, 121
symbols. *See also* imagery
in alchemy, 48–52, 68–69
in *Ars magna,* 74–75
geometric, 53–54
pelican, 48–49
of transformation, 70–71

uroboros as, 46
yin-yang, 33–34

T

tabula rasa (blank slate), 108
tail-eater. *See uroboros*
"take apart, put together," 6, 80–81,
146
in alchemy, 66–76
in chaos theory, 77–88
tamas (downward movement), 90
Tao Te Ching (Lao Tzu), 53
teleology, 56, 64
temenos (enclosed sacred space), 139
Thoth, 23
Timaeus (Plato), 26–27, 45–46
time, 11, 17, 78
torus attractors, 82
transformation. *See also* self-
transformation
chaos theory in, 139
inner and outer, 1, 2
triangle, 74
Turing, Alan, 57
Turing machine, 57–58
two-body problem, 16

U

ultimate reality, 96
uncertainty principle, 135
"Union with God," 140
universe, models of, 15–16
unpredictability, 19, 103, 105–6, 111
unus mundus (unitary world), 95
uroboros, 5, 44–51, 63–64, 146

V

Varela, Francisco, 137–39
Vesalius, Andreas, 30

Index

Quest Books

encourages open-minded inquiry into
world religions, philosophy, science, and the arts
in order to understand the wisdom of the ages,
respect the unity of all life, and help people explore
individual spiritual self-transformation.

Its publications are generously supported by
The Kern Foundation,
a trust committed to Theosophical education.

Quest Books is the imprint of
the Theosophical Publishing House,
a division of the Theosophical Society in America.
For information about programs, literature,
on-line study, membership benefits, and international centers,
see www.theosophical.org
or call 800-669-1571 or (outside the U.S.) 630-668-1571.

Related Quest Titles

The Alchemist and the Path of Integration (DVD), by Martin Leiderman
Gnosticism, by Stephan A. Hoeller
The Golden Thread, by Joscelyn Godwin
Head and Heart, by Victor Mansfield
Science and the Sacred, by Ravi Ravindra
Spiritual Lessons of Chaos (DVD), by Patricia Monaghan
The Visionary Window, by Amit Goswami

To order books or a complete Quest catalog,
call 800-669-9425 or (outside the U.S.) 630-665-0130.

PRAISE FOR *INDRA'S NET*

"As in alchemy, so in chaos theory, and so also in personal transformation. Robertson brings together three complex and enigmatic processes with a simplicity and ease of which only a true adept is capable."

—**Charles Zeltzer, Ph.D.**, Jungian analyst

"Robin Robertson has a knack for grasping the pure quill in our crazy-making, daily whirl. *Indra's Net* is magical, because readers will learn more about themselves than about Indra, alchemy or chaos theory."

—**Daryl Sharp**, Jungian analyst; publisher, Inner City Books

"I would place this book, along with Ralph Abraham's *Chaos, Gaia, Eros* and Ivars Peterson's *Newton's Clock*, as the most important and enjoyable books on the history and implications of chaos theory."

—**Fred Abraham, Ph.D.**, Cofounder of the Society for Chaos Theory in Psychology; coauthor of *A Visual Introduction to Dynamical Systems Theory for Psychology*

"Elegant descriptions, up-to-date analogies, and personal reflections enrich and enliven Robertson's unfolding themes. He synthesizes alchemic mystery, mathematics, and psyche with profound simplicity, reaffirming his mastery of this genre."

—**Barry Jeromson, Ph.D.**, has taught philosophy and Jungian studies at the University of South Australia

"Robertson articulates with an uncommon clarity and erudition both modern chaos theory and alchemy . . . to foster an original contribution to our understanding of change in our souls. This jewel of a book illuminates the unpredictable detours of individuation."

—**Christophe Le Mouël, Ph.D.**, Executive Director, C.G. Jung Institute of Los Angeles

"No one on the planet today knows more than Robertson about the confluence of currents of transformation coming together from the intersection of Jungian individuation, nonlinear dynamical mathematics, and the sheer joy and magic of living fully. . . . The reader cannot but be imbued with the rich experience of metaphysical, developmental, and spiritual insight on every page."

—**Jeffrey Goldstein, Ph.D.**, Trustee of *Nonlinear Dynamics, Psychology, and Life Sciences*; Editor-in-Chief of *Emergence: Complexity and Organization*